House Beautiful

Welcome to the Table

House Beautiful

Welcome to the Table

SIMPLE RECIPES FOR GRACIOUS DINNERS & PARTIES

BARBARA SCOTT-GOODMAN
PHOTOGRAPHS BY COLIN COOKE

HEARST BOOKS
A Division of Sterling Publishing Co., Inc.
New York

Food Stylist: Andrea Kapsales
Prop Stylist: Phyllis Asher
Design by Barbara Scott-Goodman

Library of Congress Cataloging-in-Publication Data Available

10 9 8 7 6 5 4 3 2 1

Published by Hearst Books
A Division of Sterling Publishing Co., Inc.
387 Park Avenue South, New York, NY 10016

House Beautiful and Hearst Books are trademarks of Hearst Communications, Inc.

www.housebeautiful.com

Distributed in Canada by Sterling Publishing
c/o Canadian Manda Group, 165 Dufferin Street
Toronto, Ontario, Canada M6K 3H6

Distributed in Australia by Capricorn Link (Australia) Pty. Ltd.
P.O. Box 704, Windsor, NSW 2756 Australia

Manufactured in China
All Rights Reserved

Sterling ISBN 13: 978-1-58816-543-5
        ISBN 10: 1-58816-543-4

For information about custom editions, special sales, premium and corporate purchases, please contact Sterling Special Sales Department at 800-805-5489 or specialsales@sterlingpub.com.

Table of Contents

introduction

Whether it's a formal sit-down dinner, a spontaneous cocktail party, or a backyard barbecue, sharing food and drink with friends and family is a most enjoyable occasion. Gatherings that bring good food and good company together enhance our lives, foster friendship, and make our long workdays worthwhile. Above all, entertaining should be fun and embarked upon with a spirit of generosity and a sense of graciousness.

And it doesn't have to be difficult. Once you decide on the type of dinner or party, the guest list, and the menu, entertaining at home is pretty easy. The most important elements to being a successful host or hostess are to plan ahead, relax, and have a good time, which imparts a feeling of warmth and hospitality to your guests.

Welcome to the Table, chock-full of delicious recipes and good ideas for all occasions, is designed to inspire readers to gather family and friends

at the table and enjoy the simple pleasure of good food shared in the spirit of friendship. Here you'll find scores of great recipes for big cocktail party buffets as well as impromptu get-togethers. Sure, we make it a breeze to throw a smashing dinner party with many courses—but we also show how to put together a casual one-dish dinner to serve informally in the kitchen. And don't forget that the main dish is just one part of a successful party mix: We offer mouthwatering appetizer, soup, salad, and side dish recipes to accompany the main course, and plenty of home-made desserts—which are always a big hit with dinner guests. All in all, this book offers a wide range of scrumptious recipes for all styles of entertaining to fit almost any timeline and budget. In addition, in the spirit of *House Beautiful*, there are Serving Style pages spread throughout the book with great tips and ideas on quick nibbles, great party foods, decorating style, and even a weekend barbecue menu.

When planning your soiree, first decide on the number of guests and the type of party you're hosting. Then flip through the recipes in this book and decide which foods you'd like to serve. If your party is a cocktail party, a good rule of thumb is ten to twelve servings of appetizers per guest; if you are serving a meal after appetizers, then plan on four or five appetizers per person. Dips and spreads with chips, vegetables, or toasted pita breads are great appetizers to include on your menu—they are quick and don't require much attention. Check out the list of salsa variations on page 57—it has lots of delicious options and may inspire you to create a mixture of your own. For full dinner parties, plan out a menu with a balance of flavors. If you're serving a potato-based soup as a starter, serve something other than potatoes, such as Asparagus with Fresh Chives and Mint (page 160) or Oven-Braised Leeks and Garlic (page 176)—or both!—on the side to add a variety of tastes to the meal.

The basic premise of modern entertaining is this: Make your guests feel welcome and at home. There is no better way to do that than to be at ease and enjoy yourself. Of course, hosting a party takes some advance planning, but most important, it takes a sense of fun and generosity that always says, "Welcome to the table!"

chapter one

Appetizers & Drinks

appetizers & drinks

Appetizers always say "welcome" to your guests, whether you're serving them on buffet-style platters or as small bites from passed-around trays. Offer your guests a variety of nibbles with a drink or glass of wine or champagne to break the ice, stimulate appetites, and get the evening off to a great start. All the appetizers in this chapter are terrific on their own or you can combine any number for a larger cocktail party spread.

Warm Citrus and Fennel Olives

Here is a delicious way to prepare olives—sauté them in olive oil over low heat with slices of fennel and orange and lemon zest. When they are warm, the olives taste rich and meaty, and their heady aroma fills the air.

Prep time: 5 minutes Cook time: 10 minutes

1 tablespoon extra-virgin olive oil
¼ cup thinly sliced fennel
1 clove garlic, thinly sliced
2 cups mixed olives
1 tablespoon orange zest
1 tablespoon lemon zest
Pinch red pepper flakes (optional)

1. Heat the oil in a skillet over medium heat. Add the fennel and garlic and cook, stirring often, until softened, about 5 minutes.

2. Add the olives with a bit of their juice and the orange and lemon zest; cook, stirring occasionally, until warmed through, about 5 minutes. Add the red pepper flakes, if you like, and cook for an additional minute. Serve with toothpicks.

Makes 2 cups

Spice-Toasted Party Pecans

Pecans baked with toasted spices are always a welcome treat; strategically place small bowls of these spicy bites around the room at a cocktail party. They're also great to have on hand as a snack when friends drop in for a drink.

Prep time: 10 minutes plus cooling Bake time: 15 minutes

> 1/2 teaspoon ground cumin
> 1/2 teaspoon chili powder
> 1/2 teaspoon garlic salt
> 1/2 teaspoon ground ginger
> 1/2 teaspoon ground cinnamon
> Pinch cayenne pepper
> 1 tablespoon olive oil
> 2 cups pecans
> Kosher salt

1. Preheat the oven to 325° F.
2. In a small bowl, combine the cumin, chili powder, garlic salt, ginger, cinnamon, and cayenne. Heat the oil in a small skillet over medium heat. Add the spice mixture and cook, stirring constantly, about 3 minutes.
3. Place the pecans in a large mixing bowl, add the spice mixture, and toss well to coat. Spread the nuts on a baking sheet; bake until toasted, 12 to 15 minutes, shaking the pan occasionally. Remove the nuts from the oven, sprinkle with salt to taste, and let cool for at least 1 hour.

Makes 2 cups

Chicken and Scallion Yakitori with Peanut Dipping Sauce

Tender little bites of marinated and grilled chicken make delicious hors d'oeuvres. The tasty peanut sauce, which can be made well ahead of time, is also good to drizzle over grilled shrimp or vegetables.

Prep time: 20 minutes plus soaking and marinating Cook time: 10 minutes

Peanut Dipping Sauce:
2 tablespoons smooth peanut butter
2 tablespoons plain low-fat yogurt
2 tablespoons soy sauce
1 tablespoon fresh lime juice
1 tablespoon finely chopped fresh ginger
1/2 teaspoon toasted sesame oil
Dash hot sauce

3 tablespoons soy sauce
3 tablespoons dry sherry
1 tablespoon sugar
1 tablespoon finely chopped garlic
1 tablespoon finely chopped fresh ginger
2 whole skinless boneless chicken breasts
   (about 1 1/2 pounds), cut into 1-inch cubes
1 bunch large scallions, white parts cut into 18 (1-inch) pieces
Corn oil, for brushing

1. Soak eighteen 9 1/2-inch bamboo skewers in water overnight.
2. To make the dipping sauce: Combine the peanut butter, yogurt, soy sauce, lime juice, ginger, sesame oil, and hot sauce in a blender and blend until very smooth. Taste and adjust the seasonings. Cover and refrigerate until ready to serve (or up to 2 days). Bring to room temperature before serving.
3. In a large nonreactive bowl, whisk together the soy sauce, sherry, sugar, garlic, and ginger. Add the chicken and toss well. Cover and marinate in the refrigerator 1 to 2 hours.

4. Thread 1 piece of chicken, 1 piece of scallion, and another piece of chicken at the top end of each skewer.

5. Prepare a medium-hot gas or charcoal grill (coals are covered with a light coating of ash and glow deep red), or preheat the broiler. If grilling, brush the rack lightly with oil. If broiling, line a baking sheet with aluminum foil and brush lightly with oil. Grill or broil the skewers 3 to 4 inches from the heat, turning and brushing occasionally, until the chicken is cooked through, 8 to 10 minutes. Serve hot or at room temperature with the Peanut Dipping Sauce.

Makes 18 skewers or 6 to 8 servings

Chorizo Bites

When chorizo slices are oven-cooked in red wine and orange juice, they make a perfect small bite to enjoy with a drink or a glass of wine. Spicy Spanish chorizo sausage used to be hard to find, but it has become more popular and is now widely available in markets.

Prep time: 15 minutes Bake time: 30 minutes

> **1 pound chorizo sausage**
> **3/4 cup dry red wine**
> **2 tablespoons orange juice**

1. Preheat the oven to 400° F.

2. Cut the sausage into 3/4-inch slices and place in a baking dish. Bake until lightly browned, about 20 minutes. With tongs, turn the sausage slices over. In a small bowl, combine the wine and orange juice; pour over the sausage. Bake 10 minutes longer.

3. Transfer the sausage to a plate or shallow bowl and drizzle with a bit of the wine mixture. Serve warm with toothpicks.

Makes 6 servings

Salsas

Salsas are excellent party fare, and they're easy and fun to make. You simply need a good knife and cutting board, and, of course, the freshest ingredients available. Although salsas are most widely known as dips for chips, they are excellent accompaniments to grilled meat, poultry, and seafood, as well as rice and other grains. Enjoy!

Tomato-Mango Salsa

By adding the sweet taste of mango, pineapple, and orange juice to chopped tomatoes and onions, you create a marvelous twist on everyday salsa. In addition to the usual chips, this is wonderful with cold shrimp.

Prep time: 10 minutes

> 4 plum tomatoes (about 1 pound), seeded
>   and chopped into 1/4-inch pieces
> 3 small or 2 large ripe mangoes, peeled and diced
> 1 medium red onion, finely chopped
> 1 medium red bell pepper, stemmed, seeded, deveined,
>   and cut into 1/4-inch pieces
> 1/4 cup chopped fresh cilantro
> 4 teaspoons minced garlic
> 1 teaspoon red pepper flakes
> 1/4 cup pineapple juice
> 1/4 cup orange juice
> 2 tablespoons white vinegar
> Juice of 1 lime

1. Combine the tomatoes, mangoes, onion, pepper, cilantro, garlic, and pepper flakes in a large nonreactive bowl and mix gently.
2. In a small bowl, whisk the pineapple juice, orange juice, vinegar, and lime juice. Add to the tomato mixture and mix gently. Cover and refrigerate for at least 1 hour (or up to 2 days). Serve chilled or at room temperature.

Makes 3 cups

Tomatillo Salsa

This delicious salsa is excellent with blue corn chips. It's also good with scrambled eggs for breakfast.

Prep time: 15 minutes plus chilling Cook time: 10 minutes

> 20 tomatillos (about 1½ pounds), husked
>
> 4 cloves garlic, peeled
>
> 1 medium red onion, cut into ¼-inch pieces
>
> 1 medium tomato, coarsely chopped
>
> ½ medium green bell pepper, stemmed, seeded, deveined, and chopped into ¼-inch pieces
>
> ⅓ cup red wine vinegar
>
> 2 tablespoons chopped fresh cilantro
>
> 1 tablespoon fresh lime juice
>
> 1 tablespoon olive oil
>
> 1 teaspoon kosher salt

1. Bring a medium pot of water to a boil and add the tomatillos. Simmer until soft, 8 to 10 minutes. Remove from the heat and let cool in the cooking water.

2. Lift the tomatillos from the cooking liquid and transfer to the bowl of a food processor fitted with a steel blade. Add the garlic and purée until very smooth. Transfer the mixture to a large bowl.

3. Add the onion, tomato, green pepper, vinegar, cilantro, lime juice, olive oil, and salt to the tomatillos and mix well. Cover and refrigerate until well chilled (or up to 3 days). Serve chilled, warm, or at room temperature.

Makes 3 cups

Zesty Clam Dip

This easy-to-make dip, made with fresh clams and red pepper, is always a hit at parties. Prepare it ahead of time and serve chilled with pita crisps and garden-fresh vegetables.

Prep time: 15 minutes   Cook time: 5 minutes

> 12 cherrystone clams, rinsed well
> ½ pound block cream cheese, softened
> ½ cup low-fat sour cream
> ½ red bell pepper, stemmed, seeded, deveined, and finely diced
> 1 to 2 teaspoons hot sauce
> 1 teaspoon celery seed
> Kosher salt and freshly ground black pepper

1. Place the clams in a large soup pot, add 2 cups of water, and bring to a boil. Cover and cook until the clams open, about 5 minutes. Discard any that do not open. Drain and let cool. When cool enough to handle, remove the clams from their shells and coarsely chop.
2. Place the clams, cream cheese, sour cream, pepper, hot sauce, celery seed, and salt and pepper to taste in a food processor. Process in short pulses until fine, but not too smooth. Taste, adjust the seasonings, and process again briefly. Scrape the dip into a bowl, cover, and refrigerate until ready to serve (or up to 2 days). Serve chilled.

Makes about 1½ cups

Roasted Red Pepper Spread

Serve this delicious spread with crisp raw vegetables or Parmesan Garlic Toasts (page 27). The flavors mellow if this is made a day ahead of time.

Prep time: 15 minutes plus chilling   Broil time: 10 minutes

2 red bell peppers, halved, stemmed, seeded, and deveined

1 tablespoon olive oil

½ pound block cream cheese, softened

¼ cup sour cream

½ red onion, coarsely chopped

¼ teaspoon Worcestershire sauce

4 drops hot sauce

Pinch cayenne pepper

2 tablespoons finely chopped fresh chives

1.   Preheat the broiler. Place the pepper halves directly on a broiler tray pan and spoon the olive oil over them. Broil, turning often, until the skins are charred. Transfer to a small paper bag and fold to seal. Set aside to let the peppers cool inside the bag. When cool, rub the charred skin from the peppers and cut them into a fine dice. Transfer to a bowl.

2.   Combine the cream cheese, sour cream, onion, Worcestershire sauce, hot sauce, and cayenne in the bowl of a food processor fitted with a steel blade; process until smooth. Scrape the mixture into the bowl with the peppers. Add the chives and mix well. Cover and refrigerate for at least 1 hour (or up to 1 day). Bring to room temperature before serving.

Makes about 1½ cups

Goat Cheese and Herb Spread

For delightful hors d'oeuvres to nibble on before dinner, serve this tangy goat cheese spread with grilled bread and an assortment of olives.

Prep time: 15 minutes plus draining

> 3/4 cup plain low-fat yogurt
> 6 ounces mild goat cheese, at room temperature
> 2 tablespoons finely chopped fresh flat-leaf parsley
> 2 tablespoons finely minced scallions
> 2 teaspoons finely chopped fresh tarragon
> Kosher salt and freshly ground black pepper

1. To make the yogurt cheese: Line a sieve with a coffee filter or cheesecloth and place over a bowl. Spoon the yogurt into the filter and let drain for about 1 hour at room temperature, or overnight in the refrigerator.

2. In a medium bowl, gently mash the goat cheese with a fork to soften. Add the parsley, scallions, and tarragon and work them in with the fork. Season with salt and pepper and mash to make a smooth, well-blended spread.

3. Add the yogurt cheese and mix until well blended. (The spread can be covered and refrigerated for up to 2 days; bring to room temperature before serving.)

Makes about 1 cup

Breads and Toasts

Although it may seem too labor-intensive to bake bread from scratch or make your own garlic toasts, the results are well worth it. And besides, who can resist the delicious fragrance and warm goodness of a loaf right from the oven?

Rosemary Focaccia

Warm focaccia, fresh from the oven, is fabulous to serve your guests with an assortment of cheeses, olives, and wine. If you are new to making yeast breads, focaccia is a great place to start. Unlike most yeast doughs, this one does not require lengthy kneading or dual risings. In fact, the dough is kneaded for only a few minutes, right in the bowl in which it's mixed.

Prep time: 20 minutes plus rising Bake time: 15 minutes

> 1½ cups lukewarm water
> 1 (¼-ounce) package (1 scant tablespoon) active dry yeast
> 2 cups bread flour
> 1½ to 2 cups unbleached all-purpose flour
> 1 tablespoon salt
> 2 tablespoons olive oil, plus more for brushing
> 1 to 2 tablespoons chopped fresh rosemary
> 1 large clove garlic, sliced
> Coarse or kosher salt

1.   Pour the water into a large ceramic or glass mixing bowl and sprinkle the yeast on top. Stir gently. Let sit until foamy, 2 to 3 minutes. Stir in the bread flour with a wooden spoon. Add 1½ cups all-purpose flour, the salt, and olive oil and stir vigorously to mix. The dough should gather together and pull away from the side of the bowl but remain sticky and moist. Add more all-purpose flour, as necessary, for the correct consistency.

2.   With lightly oiled or floured hands, knead the dough gently in the bowl 2 to 3 minutes, until smooth. Rub the dough on all sides with a little olive oil. Cover the bowl with a towel or plastic wrap and let rise in a warm place 45 minutes to 1 hour, until doubled.

3. Preheat the oven to 400° F. Lightly oil a baking sheet with olive oil. (Oil 2 sheets if making 2 small loaves.) Using your fist, gently punch the dough down in the bowl. Lift from the bowl and place on the oiled sheet. (If making 2 loaves, divide the dough in half and place one half on each sheet.) With lightly oiled fingertips, stretch the dough until it is about 1/4-inch thick. The loaf or loaves should be free-form and rustic looking.

4. Using your fingertips, make indentations randomly in the stretched dough, breaking through the dough to form craters and tears about 1 inch long. Brush the dough with olive oil, letting it pool in some of the indentations. Sprinkle with the rosemary, garlic, and salt to taste.

5. Bake the focaccia 15 to 20 minutes, until lightly brown. Serve while still warm, breaking off pieces for eating.

Makes 1 large or 2 small loaves, or 10 to 12 servings

Parmesan Garlic Toasts

Prep time: 10 minutes Bake time: 4 minutes

> 1 loaf French or Italian bread, cut into 12 (1-inch-thick) slices
>
> 6 cloves garlic, halved
>
> 3 to 4 tablespoons extra-virgin olive oil
>
> 2 to 3 tablespoons freshly grated Parmesan cheese

Preheat the oven to 350° F. Rub each slice of bread generously with garlic and place on a baking sheet. Brush the olive oil on the bread slices and sprinkle with the Parmesan. Bake 3 to 4 minutes, until golden brown. Serve immediately.

Makes 6 servings

Serving Style

Whether you are making appetizers from scratch or serving up a spread of store-bought treats, always serve them with style. The only rule is to do what best fits your time frame and your mood.

WINE & CHEESE

When buying cheese, think in terms of taste, texture, and contrast. Choose a few cheeses from different categories: hard, semi-hard, and soft-ripened. Have fun with your guests trying different pairings of wine and cheese. The possibilities are endless. And don't be afraid to make additions to the cheese plate—cheese looks and tastes wonderful with fresh fruit and fruit spreads.

crostini & cocktails

Crostini are little rounds of bread that have been brushed with olive oil and lightly baked or toasted until crisp. They are excellent to serve at cocktail parties or as a delightful nibble before a sit-down dinner. They can be served with an assortment of dips and spreads; in addition to the recipes on pages 33–35, here are a few good ideas for topping crostini.

- Roasted fennel and black olives

- Roasted zucchini and Parmesan cheese

- Roasted asparagus and Parmesan cheese

- Sautéed Swiss chard and prosciutto

- Sautéed spinach and ricotta cheese

- Sautéed watercress and ham

- Sautéed broccoli rabe and mozzarella cheese

- Grilled eggplant and roasted red peppers

- Mozzarella cheese and anchovies

- Ricotta cheese, chopped tomatoes and basil

- Goat cheese and black olive tapenade

- Warm white beans and sautéed Swiss chard

- Puréed chickpeas and roasted red onions

- Puréed fava beans and roasted red peppers

Bruschetta and Crostini

Bruschetta and crostini are perfect to serve at intimate get-togethers as well as big cocktail parties. Below are a few favorites—no matter which ones you choose to serve as delicious nibbles, they all say, "Welcome to the table."

Bruschetta is thick slices of country bread that are grilled or baked, rubbed with garlic, and brushed with olive oil. Any number of toppings can be added to bruschetta—chopped tomatoes, grilled eggplant, fennel, sautéed spinach or Swiss chard, prosciutto, mozzarella, ricotta, or Parmesan cheese. The combinations and possibilities are endless.

Crostini are usually smaller than bruschetta (crostini means "little toasts" in Italian). Sliced rounds from a baguette are brushed with olive oil and lightly toasted or baked. They are delicious with many kinds of toppings—chicken liver mousse, tapenade, crabmeat salad, hummus, or soft cheese spread, to name just a few.

Bruschetta

Bruschetta can be prepared on a charcoal grill, in a grill pan, or in the oven. Cook as many slices as will fit in a single layer and turn them once; they are perfect when they are golden brown and crispy.

Prep time: 10 minutes Grill time: 5 minutes

> 6 (¾-inch-thick) slices country bread
> 3 large cloves garlic, halved
> Olive oil, for brushing
> Topping of choice (recipes follow)

1. Prepare a charcoal fire or heat a grill pan over medium heat. Grill the bread slices in a single layer, turning once, until they are golden brown, crispy, and slightly charred around the edges, 3 to 5 minutes. (To prepare bruschetta in the oven, arrange the bread slices in a single layer on a baking sheet; bake in a 450°F oven until golden brown and crispy, 6 to 8 minutes.)
2. Rub garlic on one side of each slice and brush lightly with olive oil. Cut each slice in half and top with desired topping.

Makes 12 bruschetta or 6 servings

SALAMI, RICOTTA, AND FENNEL TOPPING

This is a fabulous combination of tastes.

Prep time: 10 minutes Cook time: 5 minutes

> 1 fennel bulb, trimmed and sliced lengthwise into 1-inch pieces
> 2 tablespoons extra-virgin olive oil
> 1 tablespoon fresh lemon juice
> 12 very thin slices salami or sopressata
> About 1/2 cup ricotta cheese, at room temperature
> Freshly ground black pepper

Bring a saucepan of salted water to a boil. Add the fennel and simmer until just tender, 3 to 5 minutes. Transfer to a bowl and toss with the olive oil and lemon juice. Top each bruschetta with a slice of salami, a little cheese, and a spoonful of the fennel. Top with freshly ground black pepper and serve.

Makes enough topping for 12 bruschetta

GOAT CHEESE, PROSCIUTTO, AND TOMATO TOPPING

Prep time: 35 minutes

> 2 medium tomatoes, finely diced
> 1 tablespoon extra-virgin olive oil
> 3/4 cup mild goat cheese, at room temperature
> 12 thin slices prosciutto

Combine the tomatoes and olive oil in a medium bowl and toss well. Let sit for at least 30 minutes. Spread each bruschetta with goat cheese, top with a slice of prosciutto, and then with a spoonful of the tomato mixture.

Makes enough topping for 12 bruschetta

WARM SPINACH AND CHICKPEA TOPPING

Prep time: 5 minutes Cook time: 10 minutes

> 2 tablespoons olive oil
>
> 3 cups baby spinach, washed well
>
> 1 (15.5-ounce) can chickpeas, rinsed and drained
>
> 2 tablespoons dry white wine
>
> Pinch dried chile flakes
>
> Kosher salt and freshly ground black pepper

1. Heat 1 tablespoon olive oil in a large skillet or sauté pan over medium heat. Add the spinach and sauté until wilted, about 3 minutes. Transfer to a bowl.

2. In the same pan, heat the remaining 1 tablespoon olive oil. Add the chickpeas, wine, chile flakes, and salt and pepper to taste. Sauté until the wine is reduced and the chickpeas are heated through, about 5 minutes.

3. Top each bruschetta with spinach and then chickpeas and serve.

Makes enough topping for 12 bruschetta

Crostini

Crostini are a snap to toast in the oven: Simply arrange baguette slices on a baking sheet and bake until lightly browned and crisp. Then take your pick from the three delightful toppings that follow, or look on page 29 for more delicious toppings.

Prep time: 5 minutes Bake time: 5 minutes

> 12 (1/2-inch-thick) slices from a baguette
> 3 large cloves garlic, halved
> Olive oil, for brushing
> Topping of choice (recipes follow)

Preheat the oven to 400° F. Arrange the bread slices in a single layer on a baking sheet and bake until golden brown and crispy, about 5 minutes. Rub garlic on one side of each slice and brush lightly with olive oil. Top the crostini with desired toppings and serve.

Makes 12 crostini or 6 servings

ROQUEFORT-WALNUT SPREAD

This quick spread tastes even better when it is made a day or two ahead of time. It's terrific on crostini—but is also very good with thin slices of pumpernickel bread.

Prep time: 10 minutes plus chilling

> 1/2 pound Roquefort or Gorgonzola cheese, at room temperature
> 1/2 pound block cream cheese, softened
> 1/4 cup heavy cream
> 1/4 cup coarsely chopped walnuts
> 2 teaspoons cognac
> Toasted walnut halves, for garnish

1. Combine the Roquefort cheese, cream cheese, and heavy cream in the bowl of a food processor fitted with a steel blade. Blend until smooth. Transfer to a mixing bowl and fold in the chopped walnuts and cognac. Cover and refrigerate until chilled (or up to 2 days).
2. Top warm crostini with the spread, garnish with walnut halves, and serve.

Makes about 2 1/2 cups or enough spread for 36 crostini

CHICKEN LIVER MOUSSE WITH RED ONION SAUCE

Easy and delicious chicken liver mousse tastes wonderful topped with a spunky onion sauce. The delectable sauce is also great with grilled burgers, pork tenderloin, and lamb chops.

Prep time: 20 minutes plus chilling Cook time: 1 hour 10 minutes

Chicken Liver Mousse:

¾ **pound chicken livers, picked over**

⅛ **teaspoon dried thyme**

⅛ **teaspoon allspice**

⅛ **teaspoon ground cinnamon**

Pinch cayenne pepper

4 **tablespoons (½ stick) unsalted butter**

½ **cup thinly sliced shallots**

¼ **pound fresh mushrooms, preferably cremini, thinly sliced**

Kosher salt and freshly ground black pepper

1 **tablespoon cognac**

Red Onion Sauce:

4 **large red onions, cut into ¼-inch dice**

3 **cups chicken broth, preferably homemade**

½ **cup dry sherry**

2 **tablespoons balsamic vinegar**

1 **tablespoon sugar**

Kosher salt and freshly ground black pepper

¾ **cup crème fraîche, low-fat sour cream, or plain yogurt**

1. To make the mousse: Place the chicken livers, thyme, allspice, cinnamon, and cayenne in a bowl and toss gently to combine. Melt the butter in a heavy skillet over medium heat. Add the shallots, mushrooms, and salt and pepper to taste. Cook, stirring often, until the mushrooms give up their liquid. Continue cooking until most of the liquid has evaporated. Add the chicken liver mixture and cook, stirring occasionally, until the livers are cooked through, 10 to 12 minutes. Remove from the heat and let cool.

2. Scrape the mixture into the bowl of a food processor fitted with a steel blade. Add the cognac and blend to a fine purée. Transfer to a bowl and let cool. Cover and refrigerate until chilled (or up to 2 days).

3. To make the sauce: In a saucepan, combine the onions, broth, sherry, vinegar, and sugar. Bring to a boil over high heat. Reduce the heat and simmer, stirring occasionally, 40 to 45 minutes, until most of the liquid evaporates. Season with salt and pepper. Stir in the crème fraîche and cook over very low heat for about 10 minutes longer, until the flavors blend. (The sauce can be covered and refrigerated for up to 1 week.) Serve warm or at room temperature.

4. Spread the Chicken Liver Mousse onto warm crostini, garnish with dollops of Red Onion Sauce, and serve.

Makes enough topping for 30 crostini

CRABMEAT, CORN, AND BLACK BEAN TOPPING

Prep time: 15 minutes

> 1 pound (2 cups) lump crabmeat, drained and picked over
>
> 1 tablespoon fresh lemon juice
>
> Kosher salt and freshly ground black pepper
>
> ¾ cup cooked corn kernels (from 1 or 2 ears fresh corn)
>
> 1 scallion, finely minced
>
> 1 tablespoon chopped fresh flat-leaf parsley
>
> 3 tablespoons mayonnaise
>
> 1 tablespoon plain yogurt
>
> Dash hot sauce
>
> ½ cup canned black beans, drained and rinsed

1. Combine the crabmeat, lemon juice, and salt and pepper to taste in a large bowl. Gently toss with a fork, mashing the crabmeat a bit. Add the corn, scallion, and parsley and toss again.

2. Mix together the mayonnaise, yogurt, and hot sauce in a small bowl. Gently fold into the crabmeat mixture. Taste and adjust the seasonings. Add the black beans and toss again. Spoon onto warm crostini and serve.

Makes about 2½ cups or enough topping for 36 crostini

Shrimp, Crab, and Avocado Cocktail

Here is a fabulous chilled seafood concoction to serve for a first course. This is also a good recipe to experiment with—try it with some lobster meat, or a few steamed baby clams, along with a handful of fresh chopped tomatoes.

Prep time: 40 minutes plus chilling Cook time: 3 minutes

1 pound medium shrimp
1 pound (2 cups) lump crabmeat, drained and picked over
1 medium red onion, finely chopped
2 scallions, finely minced
2 tablespoons fresh lemon juice
2 tablespoons fresh lime juice
2 tablespoons extra-virgin olive oil
2 tablespoons chopped fresh cilantro
Kosher salt and freshly ground black pepper
Dash hot sauce
1 Hass avocado, peeled, pitted, and cut into small chunks

1. Bring a large pot of salted water to a boil. Add the shrimp and cook until pink and cooked through, 3 to 4 minutes. Drain and run under cold water; peel and devein.
2. In a large bowl, combine the shrimp, crabmeat, onion, and scallions and gently toss together. Sprinkle with the lemon juice, lime juice, and olive oil and toss again. Stir in the cilantro and season with salt and pepper. Cover and refrigerate for about 1 hour.
3. Gently stir the hot sauce into the seafood mixture. Gently fold in the avocado. Spoon into 8-ounce glasses and serve immediately.

Makes 6 to 8 servings

Pickled Shrimp

These briny shrimp are excellent to serve with drinks or as part of a cocktail party buffet. They can be made ahead of time since they marinate for a day or two before serving.

Prep time: 30 minutes plus chilling Cook time: 13 minutes

    1 cup tarragon vinegar
    1/2 cup water
    6 slices fresh ginger
    2 tablespoons coriander seeds
    1 tablespoon fennel seeds
    1 tablespoon mixed peppercorns
    2 1/2 pounds large shrimp
    1 red onion, thinly sliced
    1 lemon, thinly sliced
    1/4 cup small capers, drained
    3 cloves garlic, thinly sliced
    Pinch cayenne pepper
    4 bay leaves
    1/4 cup extra-virgin olive oil
    Kosher salt and freshly ground black pepper

1. In a medium nonreactive saucepan, combine the vinegar, water, ginger, coriander seeds, fennel seeds, and peppercorns. Bring to a boil over medium-high heat. Reduce the heat and simmer 10 minutes. Set aside and let cool completely.
2. Meanwhile, bring a large pot of salted water to a boil. Add the shrimp. Remove from the heat and let stand until the shrimp are pink and cooked through, about 3 minutes. Drain, rinse, and let cool completely. Shell and devein the shrimp.
3. In a large glass or ceramic bowl, combine the shrimp, onion, lemon, capers, garlic, cayenne, and bay leaves; gently toss. Whisk the olive oil and salt and pepper to taste into the pickling mixture, then add to the shrimp mixture. Cover tightly and marinate in the refrigerator for at least 24 hours (or up to 3 days).
4. To serve, with a slotted spoon, transfer the shrimp to a platter; serve cold or at room temperature with toothpicks.

Makes 6 to 8 servings

Red Snapper, Bell Pepper, and Tomato Ceviche

Ceviche is a cold preparation of fish or shellfish that has been "cooked" by marinating in citrus juice. It is excellent served with tortilla chip scoops or grilled bread. Be sure to prepare this with the freshest snapper you can find and have your fishmonger fillet and skin the fish for you. The ceviche can also be made with fresh grouper, flounder, or sea bass.

Prep time: 20 minutes plus chilling

1½ pounds red snapper fillets, skinned
    and cut into ¼-inch cubes
¾ cup fresh lemon juice (from about 4 lemons)
¾ cup fresh lime juice (from 6 to 8 limes)
½ cup diced red onion
2 scallions, finely minced
½ cup diced red bell pepper
½ cup diced yellow bell pepper
1 jalapeño chile pepper, seeded, deveined, and minced
½ cup diced plum tomato
¼ cup chopped green olives
2 tablespoons chopped fresh flat-leaf parsley
1 tablespoon capers, drained
2 teaspoons extra-virgin olive oil
Dash hot sauce
Kosher salt and freshly ground black pepper
2 bunches watercress, rinsed and stemmed

1. In a nonreactive bowl, combine the fish, lemon juice, and lime juice; mix well. Cover and marinate in the refrigerator, stirring occasionally, 6 hours.

2. In a medium bowl, combine the onion, scallions, bell peppers, jalapeño, tomato, olives, parsley, capers, olive oil, hot sauce, and salt and pepper to taste; mix well. Cover and refrigerate 6 hours.

3. Just before serving, drain the fish, discarding the liquid, and transfer to a large bowl. Add the bell pepper and tomato mixture and mix well. Taste and adjust the seasonings. Arrange the watercress on a large platter. Spoon the ceviche on top and serve immediately.

Makes 8 to 10 servings

Corn Pancakes with Smoked Salmon and Watercress Sauce

These elegant pancakes topped with smoked salmon and delicate watercress sauce are a perfect starter for a special holiday party.

Prep time: Sauce: 20 minutes; Pancakes: 15 minutes Cook time: 30 minutes

Watercress Sauce:
1 bunch watercress, rinsed and stemmed
½ tablespoon unsalted butter
1 tablespoon chopped shallot
2 tablespoons dry white wine
2 tablespoons chicken broth
⅔ cup heavy cream
Kosher salt and freshly ground black pepper

Corn Pancakes:
3 large eggs
3 tablespoons unbleached all-purpose flour
Kosher salt
1½ cups cooked corn kernels (from 3 or 4 ears fresh corn)
3 to 4 tablespoons corn oil

6 ounces smoked salmon
Snipped fresh chives, for garnish

1. To make the sauce: Bring a pot of salted water to a boil. Add the watercress and cook until just tender, about 1 minute. Drain and rinse; with your hands, squeeze out all the excess moisture. Coarsely chop. In a small saucepan, melt the butter over medium heat. Add the shallot and sauté until golden, about 1 minute. Add the wine and broth; cook until almost completely reduced. Add the cream and bring to a boil; reduce the heat, and simmer, stirring frequently, for about 3 minutes. Stir in the watercress and salt and pepper to taste. Transfer to a food processor and blend until smooth. The sauce should be very light and creamy. (The sauce can be made ahead of time. It will keep, covered, in the refrigerator, for up to 2 days.) Bring to room temperature before serving.

2. To make the pancakes: Combine the eggs, flour, and salt to taste in the bowl of a food processor fitted with a steel blade. Blend well, taste, and adjust the seasonings. Transfer the batter to a mixing bowl. Stir in the corn.

3. Heat 2 tablespoons oil in a large skillet or sauté pan until hot. With a tablespoon measure, ladle the batter into the pan to make 4 to 6 pancakes, flattening the batter with the back of the spoon. Cook until golden brown on the bottom, about 2 minutes. Turn the pancakes over and cook until golden on the other side, about 2 minutes longer. Repeat with the remaining batter, adding more oil as needed. Transfer the pancakes to a warm oven (200° F) as they are cooked.

4. Place a 2-inch piece of smoked salmon on each pancake and drizzle with Watercress Sauce. Garnish with chives and serve immediately.

Makes 24 pancakes, about 6 to 8 servings

Chilled Mussels
with Mustard Vinaigrette

This is a fine way to serve mussels for a party. Prince Edward Island mussels are a favorite—they are small and clean and have a wonderful briny taste.

Prep time: 30 minutes Cook time: 12 minutes

  2 tablespoons olive oil
  3 cloves garlic, thinly sliced
  1 1/2 cups dry white wine
  2 pounds mussels (about 32 per pound),
    scrubbed, debearded, and rinsed

  Mustard Vinaigrette:
  1/2 small onion, chopped
  1/4 cup chopped fresh flat-leaf parsley
  2 cloves garlic, finely chopped
  1/4 cup dry white wine
  1 1/2 tablespoons white vinegar
  2 teaspoons Dijon mustard
  1 teaspoon Worcestershire sauce
  Dash hot sauce
  Kosher salt and freshly ground black pepper
  1/3 cup olive oil
  1/3 cup corn oil

1.   Heat the olive oil in a large soup pot over medium heat. Add the sliced garlic and sauté 2 minutes. Add the wine and bring to a boil. Add the mussels, reduce the heat, cover, and cook until the mussels open, 6 to 8 minutes. Using a slotted spoon, transfer the mussels to a bowl. Discard any unopened or broken mussels. Set aside to cool.

2.   When cool enough to handle, remove the mussels from their shells, transfer to a bowl, and refrigerate. Reserve half the mussel shells.

GONE FISHING

Fresh mussels will last a couple of days if they are properly cared for. To test for freshness, check the shells. They should be closed. If open they should close easily when tapped. If they don't, don't eat them.

3. To make the vinaigrette: Combine the onion, parsley, garlic, wine, vinegar, mustard, Worcestershire, hot sauce, and salt and pepper to taste in the bowl of a food processor fitted with a steel blade. Blend until smooth. With the machine running, add the olive oil and corn oil very slowly in a thin, steady stream, blending constantly. Continue blending until the oils are thoroughly incorporated into the vinaigrette.

4. Pour about $1/2$ cup vinaigrette over the chilled mussels and toss gently. Add more vinaigrette as needed.

5. Spoon 2 mussels into each mussel shell and arrange on a serving platter. Cover and refrigerate until ready to serve (up to 3 hours).

Makes 32 pieces or 8 servings

Cocktails

It's always easy to pour a glass of wine or a beer for your guests, but why not make the cocktail hour a little more interesting and fun with these recipes for festive, thirst-quenching cocktails? Your company will be glad you did.

Raspberry Champagne Cocktails

This is a lovely, sophisticated way to start the evening.

Prep time: 35 minutes

> 1 cup fresh raspberries, plus 6 plump berries for garnish
> 3 tablespoons (1½ ounces) crème de cassis
> 2 tablespoons superfine sugar
> 1 (750-ml) bottle champagne or sparkling wine, chilled

1. Place the raspberries, crème de cassis, and sugar in a blender and process until smooth. Refrigerate 30 minutes.

2. Spoon 2 heaping teaspoons purée into each of 6 champagne flutes. Slowly add the champagne, giving the bubbles a chance to subside a little before completely filling glass. Garnish with raspberries and serve immediately.

Makes 6 servings

Fresh Citrus Mimosas

Here is an excellent version of the traditional mimosa.

Prep time: 15 minutes

> 12 oranges
> 3 pink or ruby red grapefruits
> 2 (750-ml) bottles champagne or sparkling water, chilled

1. Squeeze the juice from the oranges and grapefruits. Combine the juices in a large pitcher. You should have about 6 cups of juice. Refrigerate until ready to serve.
2. Fill champagne flutes halfway with the juice. Add an equal amount of champagne. Serve immediately.

Makes 12 mimosas or 6 servings

Fruity Sangria

Sangria made with fresh fruit is a delicious and refreshing cooler to serve on a warm summer evening. Take full advantage of the very good and affordable Spanish red wines that are now on the market—they're perfect for making Sangria.

Prep time: 10 minutes plus chilling Cook time: 5 minutes

Citrus Syrup:
1 cup sugar
1/2 cup water
Zest of 1 orange
Zest of 1 lemon
1 cinnamon stick

1 (750-ml) bottle full-bodied Spanish red wine
1/4 cup (2 ounces) brandy
1/2 orange, thinly sliced
1/2 lemon, thinly sliced
1 peach, peeled, pitted, and thinly sliced (optional)
8 fresh strawberries (optional)

1. To make the syrup: Combine the sugar, water, orange zest, and lemon zest in a saucepan and bring to a boil over high heat. Reduce the heat, add the cinnamon stick, and simmer, stirring with a wooden spoon, about 5 minutes, until the sugar dissolves; let cool slightly. Strain into a lidded glass jar or similar container. Cool completely, cover, and refrigerate.
2. Combine the wine, brandy, and 1/4 cup syrup in a pitcher and stir (reserve the remaining syrup for later batches of sangria). Add the orange slices, lemon slices, peach slices, and strawberries, if using, and stir. Refrigerate 2 to 3 hours or until ready to serve. Pour over ice in tall glasses.

Makes 6 servings

Campari and Orange Juice Cocktails

Ruby-red Campari and fresh-squeezed orange juice make a beautiful and elegant aperitif to serve to your guests anytime.

Prep time: 5 minutes

>   1½ cups (12 ounces) Campari
>   3 cups freshly squeezed orange juice
>   Club soda or seltzer
>   Orange slices, for garnish

Combine the Campari and orange juice in a large pitcher and stir well. Pour over ice in 6 highball glasses; add a splash of club soda or seltzer to each glass and garnish with an orange slice.

Makes 6 servings

Cosmos for a Crowd

Cosmos are quite a popular way to begin a party, but one drawback to making them is the time spent squeezing so many limes. However, frozen limeade works very well instead. Very easy, and very tasty!

Prep time: 10 minutes

>   4 cups limeade, made from frozen concentrate
>   2 cups (16 ounces) vodka
>   1 cup cranberry juice
>   ½ cup (4 ounces) Triple Sec
>   Lime slices, for garnish

Combine the limeade, vodka, cranberry juice, and Triple Sec in a lidded glass jar or similar container; cover and shake well. Refrigerate until well chilled. Before serving, shake again, then transfer to a large glass pitcher. Pour into martini glasses garnished with lime slices.

Makes 12 to 14 servings

Lemonade Coolers

Try this incredibly refreshing drink during warm weather days. It's delicious when made with commercial pink or yellow lemonade, but for something really special, try it with homemade lemonade.

Prep time: 5 minutes

> 4 cups Homemade Lemonade (recipe below)
>   or store-bought lemonade
> 1 cup (8 ounces) vodka
> ¼ cup chopped fresh mint
> Lemon slices, for garnish
> Mint leaves, for garnish

Combine the lemonade, vodka, and mint into a large pitcher; stir well. Pour over ice in tall glasses and garnish with lemon slices and mint leaves.

Makes 6 servings

HOMEMADE LEMONADE

Prep time: 10 minutes plus chilling Cook time: 5 minutes

> 4 cups sugar
> 2 cups water
> ½ cup fresh lemon juice (from 2 to 3 lemons)
> 1 quart cold water

1. To make the syrup: Combine the sugar and water in a saucepan and bring to a boil over high heat. Reduce the heat and simmer, stirring with a wooden spoon, about 5 minutes, until the sugar dissolves. Let cool slightly. Transfer to a lidded glass jar or similar container. Cool completely, cover, and refrigerate until ready to serve (or up to 3 weeks).
2. In a large pitcher, combine ½ cup sugar syrup, the lemon juice, and water and mix well. Chill in the refrigerator for at least 1 hour.

Makes 1 quart

Lime Sea Breezes

Sea Breezes are usually made with vodka, but they're also mighty good with white rum and lots of fresh lime juice.

Prep time: 5 minutes

> **3 cups cranberry juice**
> **²/₃ cup grapefruit juice**
> **Juice of 1 lime**
> **1 cup (8 ounces) white rum**
> **Lime slices, for garnish**

Combine the cranberry juice, grapefruit juice, lime juice, and rum in a large pitcher and stir well. Pour over ice in highball glasses and garnish with lime slices.

Makes 6 servings

Classic Daiquiris

It is said that an American engineer working near the town of Daiquiri, Cuba, invented the daiquiri at the turn of the 20th century. Since then, there have been many variations of the drink. This is the classic.

Prep time: 10 minutes plus cooling Cook time: 5 minutes

Syrup:
1 cup sugar
1/2 cup water

1 1/2 cups (12 ounces) light rum
1/4 cup fresh lime juice (from 2 to 3 limes)
Ice

1. To make the syrup, combine the sugar and water in a saucepan and bring to a boil over high heat. Reduce the heat and simmer, stirring with a wooden spoon, about 5 minutes, until the sugar dissolves. Let cool slightly. Transfer to a lidded glass jar or similar container. Cool completely, cover, and refrigerate until ready to serve (or up to 3 weeks).
2. Combine the rum, lime juice, and 1 tablespoon plus 1 teaspoon syrup in a blender (reserve the remaining syrup for another batch of daiquiris). Add ice to fill the blender, and blend until the ice is crushed. Pour the daiquiris into cocktail glasses and serve immediately.

Makes 6 servings

Fresh Berry Daiquiris

Whip up a pitcher of daiquiris made with summer-fresh berries in any combination.

Prep time: 10 minutes plus cooling Cook time: 5 minutes

Syrup:
1 cup sugar
1/2 cup water

1 1/2 cups (12 ounces) light rum
1 cup fresh blueberries, rinsed and drained
1 cup strawberries or blackberries, rinsed and sliced
1 sliced banana
1/4 cup fresh lemon juice
Ice

1. To make the syrup: Combine the sugar and water in a saucepan and bring to a boil over high heat. Reduce the heat and simmer, stirring with a wooden spoon, about 5 minutes, until the sugar dissolves. Let cool slightly. Transfer to a lidded glass jar or similar container. Cool completely, cover, and refrigerate until ready to serve (or up to 3 weeks).
2. Combine the rum, berries, banana, lemon juice, and 3 tablespoons of the syrup in a blender (reserve the remaining syrup for another batch of daiquiris). Add ice to fill the blender, and blend until the mixture is frothy and the ice is crushed. Pour the daiquiris into a large pitcher or cocktail glasses and serve immediately.

Makes 6 servings

Bloody Marys with Fresh Horseradish

The Bloody Mary is a favorite drink of many—equally beloved by tailgaters, ladies who lunch, and weekend guests. This knockout version is laced with fresh horseradish and lemon.

Prep time: 10 minutes

   1 cup canned crushed tomatoes with juice
   3 tablespoons thinly sliced red onion
   2 cloves garlic, thinly sliced
   3 tablespoons Worcestershire sauce
   2 tablespoons white vinegar
   2 tablespoons hot sauce
   1 tablespoon prepared horseradish
   1 tablespoon thinly sliced pimiento (canned roasted peppers)
   1 teaspoon sugar
   Pinch red pepper flakes
   Kosher salt and freshly ground black pepper
   3 cups tomato juice
   3/4 cup (6 ounces) vodka
   Juice of 1/3 lemon
   Freshly grated horseradish, for garnish
   6 lemon slices, for garnish

1.   Combine the canned tomatoes and their juice, onion, garlic, Worcestershire sauce, vinegar, hot sauce, prepared horseradish, pimiento, sugar, and pepper flakes in a blender or food processor fitted with a steel blade. Season with salt and pepper. Blend or process until smooth. Pour into a large pitcher.

2.   Add the tomato juice, vodka, and lemon juice and stir well. Pour over ice in large glasses and garnish with fresh horseradish and lemon slices.

Makes 6 servings

Variations
Bloody Maria: Use tequila and lime slices instead of vodka and lemon.
Danish Mary: Use aquavit instead of vodka.
Virgin Mary: Omit the vodka.

Serving Style

Serve seasonal drinks and appetizers with casual style during the summer months so you can relax and enjoy the splendid tastes of the season with friends and family.

BLENDER DRINKS

Take full advantage of summer's bounty and make delicious smoothies and cocktails in the blender. Look for the freshest and best fruit at your local farm stand or market and let your imagination take over. Think canteloupe coolers, strawberry-banana smoothies, or watermelon daiquiris.

salsa variations

Salsas can be made with many ingredients other than the usual chopped tomatoes and chile peppers. With so many intriguing fruits and vegetables on the market, it's a cinch to create new and interesting versions. Crisp tortilla chips and raw vegetables, along with frosty margaritas, chilled beer, or wine, are just right with any of these delicious variations.

- Guacamole Salsa: avocado, tomato, bell pepper, and corn

- Mango-Tomatillo Salsa: mango, tomatillo, bell pepper, and red onion

- Orange, Red Pepper & Chipotle Salsa: orange segments, red pepper, chipotle pepper, and red onion

- Pineapple-Jicama Salsa: pineapple, jicama, bell pepper, and orange juice

- Grilled Vegetable Salsa: grilled eggplant, zucchini, onion, and corn

- Tomato & Grilled Corn Salsa: tomato, grilled corn, and chile pepper

chapter two

Soups

soups

Few dishes give us a greater sense of well-being than a good soup. Whether served as a meal in itself, thick and hearty on a cold winter night, or chilled and laced with fresh herbs on a hot summer day, there is no better way to say, "Welcome to the table," than to serve a well-made, delicious soup.

Green Market Vegetable Soup

This recipe uses the best of late summer's harvest when tomatoes, zucchini, corn, and green beans are overflowing at green markets and farm stands. Quality Parmesan cheese adds wonderful, robust flavor to this soup.

Prep time: 10 minutes plus soaking Cook time: 1 hour 35 minutes

½ cup dried great Northern beans
2 tablespoons olive oil
1 medium onion, thinly sliced
2 cloves garlic, thinly sliced
2 carrots, peeled and diced
2 ribs celery, diced
4 cups chicken or vegetable broth, preferably homemade
2 cups water
2 large tomatoes, coarsely chopped with their juice
4 small new potatoes, cut into ¼-inch dice
1 small zucchini, peeled and cut into ¼-inch dice
1 cup corn kernels (from 2 large ears fresh corn)
1 cup green beans, trimmed and cut into 1-inch pieces
½ cup chopped fresh parsley
Kosher salt and freshly ground black pepper
Freshly grated Parmesan cheese, for serving

1. Pick over the beans to remove any small stones or debris; rinse thoroughly. Place in a large bowl, add enough cold water to cover by 2 inches, and soak 6 to 8 hours or overnight. Drain and place in a large saucepan; add water to cover and a pinch of salt. Bring to a boil over high heat; reduce the heat. Cover and simmer, skimming any foam that rises to the surface, 50 to 60 minutes, until just tender. Drain and set aside.
2. Heat the olive oil in a large soup pot over medium-high heat. Add the onion and garlic and cook about 5 minutes, until softened. Add the carrots and celery, cover, and cook about 10 minutes, until tender.

3. Add the broth and water and bring to a boil; reduce the heat. Add the tomatoes, potatoes, and zucchini and simmer, stirring occasionally, 20 minutes. Stir in the reserved beans, corn, and green beans and cook 10 minutes. (At this point the soup can be covered and refrigerated for up to 24 hours or 1 day; gently reheat over medium heat before serving.)
4. Just before serving the soup, stir in the parsley and season to taste with salt and pepper. Ladle into soup bowls and serve with freshly grated Parmesan cheese.

Makes 6 to 8 servings

Bloody Mary Gazpacho

This uncooked cold soup is a real summer refresher! Be sure to make it a day ahead of time to give the flavors time to blend and intensify and the soup to chill.

Prep time: 15 minutes plus chilling

3 cups Bloody Mary mix
3 cups tomato juice
1/2 cup fresh lime juice (from 4 or 5 limes)
1/2 cup extra-virgin olive oil
4 large ripe tomatoes, peeled, and finely diced
1 medium red bell pepper, stemmed, seeded, deveined, and finely chopped
1 medium yellow bell pepper, stemmed, seeded, deveined, and finely chopped
2 medium kirby cucumbers, peeled, seeded, and finely diced
1 medium red onion, finely diced
2 scallions, finely minced
3 jalapeño chile peppers, seeded, deveined, and finely diced
1 tablespoon minced garlic
2 teaspoons ground cumin, plus more if needed
Kosher salt and freshly ground black pepper
1 cup plain low-fat yogurt
2 Hass avocados, peeled, pitted, and sliced

1. In a large bowl, combine the Bloody Mary mix, tomato juice, lime juice, olive oil, tomatoes, red and yellow peppers, cucumbers, onion, scallions, jalapeño peppers, and garlic. In batches if necessary, blend one-half of the mixture in a blender until smooth. Return to the bowl and mix well. Season with 1 teaspoon cumin and salt and pepper. Cover and refrigerate 24 hours.

2. Before serving the gazpacho, stir the remaining teaspoon of cumin into the yogurt and mix well. Stir the soup well, taste, and adjust the seasonings with additional salt, pepper, and cumin if necessary. Place the avocado slices in large, shallow soup bowls, spoon the gazpacho over them, and garnish with large spoonfuls of yogurt.

Makes 6 to 8 servings

Chilled Zucchini Soup

Cool, smooth zucchini soup flavored with lemon zest, fresh herbs, and paprika is a wonderful first course for a summer night's dinner.

Prep time: 15 minutes plus chilling Cook time: 25 minutes

2 tablespoons olive oil

1/2 cup thinly sliced shallots

4 medium zucchini, peeled, halved lengthwise,
   and cut into 1/4-inch slices

1 tablespoon grated lemon zest

Kosher salt and freshly ground black pepper

2 1/2 cups chicken broth

1 1/2 cups water

1 cup chopped fresh flat-leaf parsley

2 tablespoons chopped fresh dill

1 teaspoon paprika

Dash hot sauce

1/2 cup plain low-fat yogurt

Lemon slices, for garnish

Dill sprigs, for garnish

1. In a large stockpot, heat the oil over medium heat. Add the shallots and cook, stirring occasionally, until softened, about 5 minutes. Add the zucchini, lemon zest, and salt and pepper to taste. Cook, stirring occasionally, until the zucchini is softened, about 7 minutes. Add the broth and water and bring to a boil. Reduce the heat and simmer until the zucchini is very tender, about 10 minutes. Set aside to cool.

2. Add the parsley, dill, paprika, and hot sauce to the soup. In batches if necessary, transfer the soup to a blender and blend until very smooth. Pour the mixture into a bowl, add the yogurt, and mix well. Cover and refrigerate until well chilled (or up to overnight).

3. Before serving, stir well, taste, and adjust the seasonings. Serve the soup garnished with lemon slices and dill sprigs.

Makes 6 to 8 servings

Serving Style

For casual get-togethers, there is nothing easier or more tasty than a simple lunch or supper with soup as the star of the meal, whether it's a sunny afternoon on the patio or a cold-weather night in front of the fire.

MIX & MATCH

A festive mix of colorful soup bowls and glasses sets just the right tone for impromptu and informal meals.

FRESH PRODUCE

Leftover cooked vegetables make an inferior soup. Always use crisp, fresh, seasonal vegetables in your soups and stocks. Think gazpacho made with tomatoes, cucumbers, and ripe red peppers from your garden or local farmstand, or chowders made with peak-of-season corn and fresh herbs.

BREADS

Soup and bread are soul mates. Be sure to serve your soups with home-made or bakery-fresh bread, focaccia, or crispy bread sticks.

Lobster, Corn, and Red Pepper Chowder

This sublime chowder, filled with sautéed vegetables, fresh corn off the cob, and lobster meat is a delicious summertime indulgence. Unlike most chowder, it's very light.

Prep time: 25 minutes Cook time: 30 minutes

> 1 or 2 lobsters (2½ to 3 pounds total)
> 3 ears fresh corn, husked
> 2 tablespoons unsalted butter
> 1 large or 2 small leeks (white and tender green parts),
>   halved, well washed, and finely minced
> 1 medium red bell pepper, stemmed, seeded, deveined,
>   and finely chopped
> 2 tablespoons unbleached all-purpose flour
> 4 cups chicken broth
> 1½ cups whole milk
> ¾ cup heavy cream
> Freshly ground black pepper
> 2 tablespoons chopped fresh flat-leaf parsley, for garnish
> 1 tablespoon chopped fresh chives, for garnish

1. To prepare the lobster: Bring an 8-quart pot three-quarters full of salted water to a vigorous boil. Plunge the lobsters headfirst into the water, cover, and cook over high heat 10 to 12 minutes. Remove the lobsters with tongs and drain. When cool enough to handle, remove the lobster meat from the shells and pick over. Cut the meat into chunks and set aside. Scrape the kernels from the corn cobs using a sharp knife, reserving the kernels and juices.

2. Melt the butter in a large soup pot over medium-high heat. Add the leeks and sauté 3 minutes. Add the red pepper and sauté 3 minutes. Add the flour and cook, stirring, 2 minutes. Stir in the broth, milk, and cream. Cook over medium heat, stirring, until the soup simmers and thickens slightly. Add the lobster, corn, and black pepper to taste and simmer, stirring often, 3 minutes longer. Ladle into soup bowls, garnish each with the parsley and chives, and serve immediately.

Makes 6 to 8 servings

Potato-Seafood Chowder

For everyone who likes seafood, this showstopper is a terrific dinner-party entrée. You can make the broth well ahead of time and refrigerate or freeze it. Add some good bread, a green salad, and chilled white wine, and you have a complete meal.

Prep time: 15 minutes Cook time: 1 hour 30 minutes

2 tablespoons olive oil

2 medium onions, thinly sliced

4 cloves garlic, thinly sliced

1 (28-ounce) can plum tomatoes

1 cup dry white wine

1 cup bottled clam juice

1 teaspoon fennel seed

1 teaspoon dried thyme

1/2 teaspoon saffron threads

2 bay leaves

Freshly ground black pepper

12 small new potatoes (about 3 pounds),
    quartered (4 to 5 cups)

24 littleneck clams, rinsed well

1 pound mussels, scrubbed, debearded, and rinsed

1/2 pound medium shrimp (at least 18 shrimp),
    peeled and deveined

1/2 cup chopped fresh parsley, plus more for garnish

1. Heat the olive oil in a large stockpot over medium-low heat. Add the onions and garlic and cook 10 to 15 minutes, until softened.

2. Add the tomatoes and their juice, the wine, clam juice, fennel seed, thyme, saffron, bay leaves, and pepper to taste. Bring to a boil and reduce the heat. Partially cover and simmer, stirring occasionally, 40 minutes. (At this point, the broth can be covered and refrigerated for up to 2 days, or frozen for up to 1 month.)

3. Place the potatoes in a large saucepan and cover with cold water. Lightly salt the water; bring to a boil over high heat. Reduce the heat to medium-low, cover, and cook 15 to 20 minutes, until the potatoes are fork tender. Drain and keep warm.

4. Bring the broth to a boil. Add the clams and mussels; cover and cook over high heat 8 to 10 minutes, adding the shrimp and parsley in the last 2 minutes of cooking, until the clams and mussels open and the shrimp turn pink. Discard the bay leaves and any unopened clams or mussels.

5. Spoon the potatoes into 6 shallow soup bowls. Ladle the seafood stew over the potatoes and garnish with parsley.

Makes 6 servings

Cream of Watercress Soup

Peppery watercress tastes fresh and lovely when made into a creamy soup—but keep in mind that the potato-based broth is so versatile, you can use it with any number of other vegetables as well. When serving the soup cold in warm weather, let it cool for about 30 minutes; cover and refrigerate until well chilled.

Prep time: 35 minutes   Cook time: 35 minutes

> 2 tablespoons olive oil
> 1 tablespoon unsalted butter
> 1 leek (white and tender green parts),
>   halved, well washed, and diced
> 2 cups thinly sliced onions (about 4 onions)
> 4 cups chicken broth, preferably homemade
> 4 cups water
> 6 russet potatoes, peeled and diced
> 2 cups rinsed, stemmed, finely chopped fresh watercress
>   (about 2 bunches)
> 1 cup milk
> 1/2 teaspoon ground nutmeg
> Kosher salt and freshly ground black pepper
> 3 tablespoons chopped flat-leaf parsley

1. In a large stockpot, heat the oil and butter over medium heat until the butter melts. Add the leek and onions and sauté, stirring occasionally, about 10 minutes, until tender. Add the broth, water, and potatoes and bring to a boil over high heat. Reduce the heat to medium-low and simmer, covered, 15 to 20 minutes, until the potatoes are fork-tender. Let cool for about 20 minutes. (At this point, the soup can be covered and refrigerated for up to 3 days or frozen for up to 1 month.)

2. Stir the watercress into the soup. In batches if necessary, transfer the soup to a food processor or blender; blend until very smooth.

3. Return the soup to the pot, add the milk, and heat over medium heat, stirring, until heated through. Stir in the nutmeg and season with salt and pepper. Stir in the parsley and serve immediately.

Makes 6 to 8 servings

Braised Fennel Soup

Fennel, also known as finocchio, is quite a versatile vegetable; it can be sautéed, roasted, or grilled, and it is also very good braised in the oven to make a a rich and aromatic soup.

Prep time: 15 minutes Cook time: 1 hour 20 minutes

3 tablespoons olive oil
2 medium fennel bulbs (about 1¼ pounds),
   trimmed, cored, and quartered
1 medium onion, coarsely chopped
1 medium Yukon Gold or other firm white potato, peeled and cubed
2 medium carrots, peeled and diced
3 cloves garlic, thinly sliced
8 sprigs fresh flat-leaf parsley
Pinch dried thyme
2 tablespoons unsalted butter, cut into small pieces
4 cups chicken or vegetable broth
2 cups water
Kosher salt and freshly ground black pepper
1 cup half-and-half
1 teaspoon Pernod

1. Preheat the oven to 350° F.
2. Coat the bottom of a large roasting pan with the olive oil. Place the fennel, onion, potato, carrots, and garlic in the pan. Add the parsley sprigs and sprinkle with the thyme. Dot with the butter. Pour the broth and water over the vegetables and season with salt and pepper. Cover the pan tightly with aluminum foil and bake for about 1 hour. Remove the foil and bake another 15 minutes, until the vegetables are very tender. If the vegetables are dry, add broth or water during last 15 minutes of baking. Let the vegetables cool in the pan.
3. In batches, transfer the vegetables to a food processor fitted with a steel blade and blend until smooth. Transfer the mixture to a large saucepan or stockpot and bring to a simmer over medium-low heat. Stir in the half-and-half and Pernod and let the soup get as hot as possible without boiling. Taste and adjust the seasonings. Ladle the soup into bowls and serve immediately.

Makes 6 to 8 servings

Roasted Autumn Vegetable Soup

Acorn squash, carrots, and parsnips are blended together to make a rich and creamy soup.

Prep time: 20 minutes   Cook time: 1 hour 30 minutes

3 acorn squash, seeded and halved

4 carrots, peeled and cut into ½-inch pieces

2 parsnips, peeled and cut into ½-inch pieces

1 onion, quartered

1 tablespoon unsalted butter

1 tablespoon light brown sugar

4 cups chicken broth

Kosher salt and freshly ground black pepper

2 cups water

½ teaspoon ground ginger

Pinch cayenne pepper

1 cup whole milk

2 tablespoons snipped fresh chives, for garnish

1.   Preheat the oven to 375° F.

2.   Place the squash halves, cut side up, in a large roasting pan and distribute the carrots, parsnips, and onion around them. Dot the vegetables with butter and sprinkle with brown sugar. Pour 1 cup broth over the vegetables and season with salt and pepper. Cover with foil and bake for about 1 hour, until the vegetables are very tender.

3.   Let the vegetables sit in the pan until cool enough to handle. Scoop the squash flesh from the skins and transfer to a stockpot; discard the skins. Add the remaining roasted vegetables, any pan juices, the water, and the remaining 3 cups broth. Bring to a boil over high heat. Reduce the heat to medium, stir in the ginger and cayenne, and simmer, uncovered, about 20 minutes, until the flavors blend. Set aside to cool for about 30 minutes.

4.   In batches, transfer the soup to a food processor or blender and blend until smooth. (At this point, the soup can be refrigerated for 2 to 3 days or frozen for up to 1 month.)

5.   In the stockpot, bring the soup to a gentle boil over medium-high heat. Add the milk and stir well. Season with salt and pepper and heat until piping hot. To serve, ladle into soup bowls and garnish with the chives.

Makes 6 to 8 servings

Black Bean Soup
with Madeira and Lemon

This thick, wonderfully rich, full-flavored soup is a favorite. Because the beans cook for more than 2$1/2$ hours, they do not need to be soaked or precooked.

Prep time: 15 minutes Cook time: 2 hours 45 minutes to 3 hours 30 minutes

1$1/2$ cups dried black beans
3 tablespoons olive oil
1 onion, chopped
3 ribs celery with leaves, chopped
6 cups chicken broth, preferably homemade
1 tablespoon celery seed
Kosher salt and freshly ground black pepper
2 tablespoons fresh lemon juice, or to taste
2 to 4 tablespoons dry Madeira or sherry, or to taste
Lemon slices for garnish
Chopped fresh parsley, for garnish

1. Pick over the beans to remove any small stones or debris; rinse thoroughly. Heat the oil in a large heavy saucepan over medium heat. Add the onion and celery and sauté 8 to 10 minutes, until tender. Add the beans and broth. Bring to a boil over high heat; reduce the heat to medium-low. Cover and simmer 2$1/2$ to 3 hours, until the beans are tender. Remove from the heat and set aside to cool for about 30 minutes.

2. In batches, transfer the beans to a food processor or blender and blend until smooth.

3. Return the puréed soup to the pan; add the celery seed and season with salt and pepper. Heat over medium heat, stirring occasionally, until the soup thickens slightly and is heated through. If it becomes too thick, add a little broth. Stir in the lemon juice and sherry. Ladle into bowls, garnish with the lemon slices and parsley, and serve.

Makes 6 servings

Potato, Leek, and Spinach Soup

This gently flavored soup looks and tastes wonderful—it's especially welcome as an opener to a winter dinner party.

Prep time: 50 minutes Cook time: 20 minutes

> 3 cups chicken broth
> 1 cup water
> 3 russet potatoes, peeled and diced
> 2 tablespoons olive oil
> 2 tablespoons unsalted butter
> 1 cup thinly sliced onions (about 2 onions)
> 2 leeks (white and tender green parts),
>   halved, well washed, and diced
> About 8 ounces fresh spinach leaves, well washed
> 1/2 teaspoon ground nutmeg
> Kosher salt and freshly ground black pepper
> 1 cup milk

1. Combine the broth, water, and potatoes in a large saucepan or stockpot. Bring to a boil; reduce the heat to medium-low. Cover and simmer about 15 minutes, until the potatoes are fork tender.

2. Meanwhile, heat the olive oil and butter in a skillet over medium heat until the butter is melted. Add the onions and leeks and sauté, stirring occasionally, about 10 minutes, until tender. Transfer to the soup pot with the broth and potatoes.

3. Stir the spinach and nutmeg into the soup. Season with salt and pepper. Cook over medium heat 1 to 2 minutes, until the spinach wilts and is tender. Remove the soup from the heat and let cool for about 30 minutes.

4. In batches if necessary, transfer the soup to a food processor or blender and blend until smooth. (At this point, the soup can be covered and refrigerated for up to 2 days or frozen for up to 1 month.)

5. Return the soup to the pot. Stir in the milk and heat over medium heat, stirring constantly, until heated through. Taste, adjust the seasonings, and serve immediately.

Makes 6 servings

Holiday Oyster Stew

Nothing could be easier or more delicious to have for Christmas Eve supper than a simple oyster stew. This main-dish soup needs only a salad, lots of crusty bread, and champagne. Happy holidays!

Prep time: 5 minutes Cook time: 8 minutes

> 2 cups whole milk
> 2 cups heavy cream
> 2 cups fresh oysters with their liquor
> Kosher salt and freshly ground black pepper
> Dash hot sauce (optional)
> 2 tablespoons unsalted butter, at room temperature
> ½ cup chopped fresh flat-leaf parsley, for garnish

1. Combine the milk and cream in a heavy-bottomed saucepan over medium heat until heated through; do not boil. Add the oysters and their liquor; bring to just a simmer and cook until the edges of the oysters just begin to curl, about 1 minute.
2. Season with salt and pepper and add the hot sauce, if you like. Stir in the butter and cook, stirring, until melted. Garnish with parsley and serve immediately.

Makes 6 servings

Serving Style

Soup served as a starter is always an elegant and special way to begin a dinner party. Homemade soup works well for all seasons: light and fresh in spring and summer; full-flavored and hearty in autumn and winter.

SERVING IT UP

Bring the soup tureen directly to the table to serve your guests—it lends intimacy to the meal.

Look for antique silver soup spoons at flea markets, yard sales, and estate sales. They add a special touch when serving soups and stews.

soup and...

There are wonderful accompaniments to enhance soup in addition to crackers and bread. For a delightful change of pace, try topping your soup with some of the following:

- Freshly made garlic croutons or cornbread croutons

- A sprinkling of chopped green, red, and yellow peppers

- Roasted or grilled fresh corn

- Diced fresh avocado or a spoonful of guacamole

- A dollop of plain yogurt or sour cream

- A dollop of pesto sauce

- Freshly grated Parmesan cheese

- A generous mix of fresh herbs such as flat-leaf parsley, basil, chives, sage, and tarragon

- A drizzle of extra-virgin olive oil or flavored oil such as walnut or hazelnut

- Lightly toasted pine nuts, walnuts, or pecans

chapter three

Salads

salads

Salads used to be a kind of culinary afterthought—not the flavorful mix of greens and other inventive ingredients that come to mind when considering them today. You can create fantastic salads for stylish meals simply by using the best-quality ingredients available, whether serving salad as appetizer, side dish, or entrée.

Mixed Greens
with Roasted Pears and Parmesan

This is a lovely formal salad to start an elegant autumn dinner party, but also nice to share around the kitchen table. Slow-roasted pears give it a deep caramelized flavor. Any kind of pear works well here, but it is especially good with ripe Red Bartletts. Use the best Parmesan cheese to garnish the salad.

Prep time: 20 minutes Roast time: 30 minutes

1 tablespoon corn oil
2 ripe pears, quartered, cored, and thinly sliced

Vinaigrette:
1/3 cup extra-virgin olive oil
2 tablespoons red wine vinegar
1 teaspoon herbes de Provence
Kosher salt and freshly ground black pepper

2 large heads endive
4 cups mixed salad greens
Shaved Parmesan cheese, for garnish

1. Preheat the oven to 350° F. Brush a baking sheet with the corn oil. Add the pears, turn to coat, and spread in an even layer. Roast until tender, about 30 minutes.
2. To make the vinaigrette: In a small bowl, whisk together the olive oil and vinegar. Add the herbs and salt and pepper to taste. Whisk well to combine.
3. Trim off the base of the endives, separate the leaves, and tear in half. Place in a large salad bowl, add the greens, and toss together.
4. Just before serving, whisk the vinaigrette and drizzle one-half over the endive and greens; toss gently to coat. Arrange on individual plates. Top with the roasted pears and drizzle with the remaining vinaigrette. Garnish with Parmesan shavings and additional ground pepper, if desired, and serve immediately.

Makes 6 servings

Mixed Greens with Port-Roasted Figs and Roquefort

Look for luscious, small ripe figs in the late summer or early fall. They're particularly good when roasted in port, and when added to a mix of greens and topped with tangy Roquefort cheese, they're outstanding. Black fig vinegar, available in specialty and gourmet markets, is especially welcome in this salad; it is definitely worth seeking out. But you can also make do with red wine or balsamic vinegar, and any quality blue cheese can be substituted for the Roquefort.

Prep time: 15 minutes Roast time: 30 minutes

> 9 small ripe figs
> 1/2 cup port
> 3 cups mixed salad greens
> 1 cup trimmed arugula, rinsed and dried
> 1 small head radicchio, outer leaves discarded,
>   inner leaves torn into small pieces
> 3 tablespoons extra-virgin olive oil
> 1 tablespoon black fig vinegar
> Kosher salt and freshly ground black pepper
> 1/2 cup crumbled Roquefort cheese

1. Preheat the oven to 350° F. Cut the figs in half lengthwise and trim the stems. Pour 1/4 cup port into a nonreactive baking dish and place the figs, cut-side up, in 1 layer in the dish. Pour the remaining port over the figs. Roast the figs, occasionally spooning with the remaining port, until softened, 30 to 35 minutes. Let cool slightly.
2. Just before serving, place the greens, arugula, and radicchio in a large salad bowl. In a small bowl, whisk together the olive oil, vinegar, and salt and pepper to taste until well combined. Drizzle one-half over the greens and toss well. Arrange the salad on 6 individual plates, top each serving with 3 fig halves, and sprinkle with the cheese. Drizzle with the remaining vinaigrette and serve immediately.

Makes 6 servings

Spinach, Tomato, and Pancetta Salad with Buttermilk Dressing

This scrumptious salad is especially delicious when baby spinach and summer tomatoes are at their peak. Pancetta is available at gourmet shops and Italian specialty stores, but regular bacon will also work well.

Prep time: 10 minutes Cook time: 7 minutes

Buttermilk Dressing:
½ cup mayonnaise
1 tablespoon white vinegar
1 tablespoon fresh lemon juice
¼ cup buttermilk
2 tablespoons chopped red onion
2 tablespoons chopped fresh parsley
2 to 3 tablespoons crumbled blue cheese
Freshly ground black pepper

¼ pound pancetta or bacon, cut into ⅛-inch slices
6 cups baby spinach
2 large ripe tomatoes, diced

1. To make the dressing: In a small bowl, whisk the mayonnaise, vinegar, and lemon juice. Add the buttermilk and whisk again. Stir in the onion, parsley, and blue cheese. Season with pepper. Taste and adjust the seasonings. (The dressing can be covered and refrigerated for up to 1 day.)
2. In a small skillet over medium heat, cook the pancetta until crisp. Drain on paper towels.
3. Just before serving, place the spinach in a shallow bowl or on a serving platter and arrange the tomatoes on top. Drizzle with the dressing and top with the pancetta. Add a bit more fresh pepper, if desired, and serve.

Makes 6 servings

Green Bean, Corn, and Basil Salad

This knockout salad with a lemony herb vinaigrette is a delicious side dish to serve with grilled fish or chicken. Or put out the salad bowl and plates and let guests serve themselves while the grill is heating.

Prep time: 15 minutes Cook time: 6 minutes

2 pounds fresh green beans, trimmed

3 ears fresh corn, husked

2 tablespoons finely chopped fresh basil

2 tablespoons finely chopped flat-leaf parsley

Juice of 1/2 lemon

1/3 cup extra-virgin olive oil

1 tablespoon balsamic vinegar

Kosher salt and freshly ground black pepper

1/4 cup pitted and halved kalamata olives

1. In a saucepan of boiling salted water, cook the beans until crisp-tender, 3 to 4 minutes. With a slotted spoon, transfer to a colander and rinse under cold running water; drain. Transfer to a large bowl and set aside.
2. In the same saucepan of boiling water, cook the corn 3 minutes; drain and cool. Scrape the kernels by holding the ears upright on a plate and scraping downward with a small sharp knife. Add the corn to the beans, along with the basil and parsley. Sprinkle with the lemon juice and toss.
3. In a small bowl, whisk together the oil and vinegar and season with salt and pepper. Drizzle over the salad and toss thoroughly. Place on a serving platter or in a shallow bowl and top with the olive halves. Serve warm, chilled, or at room temperature.

Makes 6 servings

Cucumber and Mint Salad

This refreshing salad is simple to make, and it complements a variety of dishes. It is excellent with grilled lamb and chicken as well as spicy dishes. The creamy yogurt dressing is a cinch to make; draining the yogurt for a few minutes makes the dressing less watery.

Prep time: 30 minutes

> 2 cups plain low-fat yogurt
> 1 teaspoon ground cumin
> Pinch red pepper flakes
> Pinch sugar
> Kosher salt and freshly ground black pepper
> 3 large cucumbers or 8 small kirby cucumbers,
>   peeled, seeded, and diced
> 1/2 red onion, finely diced
> 1/2 cup chopped fresh mint

1. Line a sieve with a coffee filter or cheesecloth and place over a bowl. Spoon the yogurt into the filter and let drain for 15 minutes. Transfer to a medium bowl and add the cumin, red pepper flakes, sugar, and salt and pepper to taste. Whisk until creamy and well combined.
2. Place the cucumbers, onion, and mint in a large bowl and toss. Drizzle with the yogurt dressing and toss again. Taste and adjust the seasonings. Cover and chill the salad for a few hours before serving.

Makes 6 servings

Roasted Beet, Orange, and Pecan Salad

Here's a beautiful salad: Sweet roasted beets, peppery arugula, and juicy oranges.

Prep time: 15 minutes plus chilling Roast time: 1 hour

3 pounds small beets (about 12), scrubbed

Tarragon Vinaigrette:
3 tablespoons white vinegar
1 tablespoon fresh lemon juice
Kosher salt and freshly ground black pepper
½ cup olive oil
2 teaspoons chopped fresh tarragon

1 bunch arugula, rinsed and stemmed
2 bunches watercress, rinsed and stemmed
2 navel oranges, peeled and cut crosswise into ¼-inch-thick slices
1 red onion, thinly sliced
½ cup pecan halves, lightly toasted (see below)

1. Preheat the oven to 375° F. Wrap 3 or 4 beets loosely in aluminum foil. Repeat with the remaining beets to make several packets. Place on a baking sheet and bake for about 1 hour, until tender when pierced with a fork. Unwrap the beets and set aside to cool. Rub off the skins and cut into quarters. Cover and refrigerate until cold, about 3 hours (or up to 1 day).
2. To make the vinaigrette: In a small bowl, combine the vinegar, lemon juice, and salt and pepper to taste and whisk well. Slowly add the olive oil in a steady stream while whisking constantly to emulsify. Whisk in the tarragon; taste and adjust the seasonings.
3. Just before serving, in a large bowl, toss together the arugula and watercress. Drizzle with one-half the vinaigrette and toss again. Arrange the greens on a large platter or 6 salad plates. Top with the beets, oranges, and onion. Drizzle with the remaining vinaigrette, sprinkle with the toasted pecan halves, and serve immediately.

Makes 6 servings

Toasting Pecans
To toast the pecans, spread on a baking sheet and toast in a 350° F oven or toaster oven about 5 minutes, until golden brown. Shake the pan once or twice for even toasting. Slide the nuts off the baking sheet onto a plate to stop the cooking and let them cool.

Serving Style

Salads make superb starters for all types of dinner parties because they lend texture and beauty to the meal. They are enticing to the eye and lighten and refresh the palate.

SALAD SERVERS

Gorgeous silver salad servers are well worth the splurge; they add a lovely grace note to the dinner when serving guests at the table.

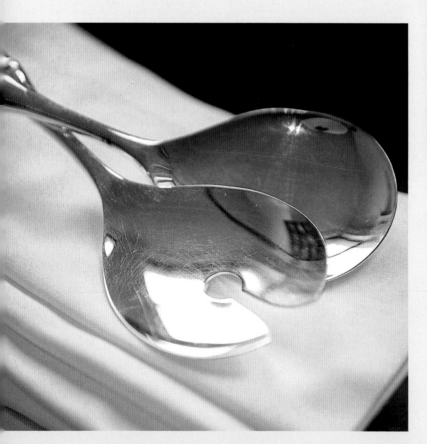

KEEP IT LIGHT

Oversize white plates are always right for serving salads. Greens, vegetables, and fruits look great on them.

oil & vinegar

OIL

Olive oil: The best olive oil for salad is extra-virgin olive oil—the result of the very first pressing of olives. It is the fruitiest and most flavorful of olive oils and the best choice for stand-out vinaigrettes.

Nut oils: Strong, aromatic oils such as walnut and hazelnut are good to combine with other oils for nutty-tasting vinaigrettes. They are also nice drizzled as a finishing touch on a salad.

VINEGAR

Red wine vinegar: Versatile red wine vinegar is made from fermented red wine. It is excellent in vinaigrettes that accompany strong-tasting greens.

Balsamic vinegar: Intense, syrupy, and with with a sweet-tart flavor, true balsamic is made in Italy from white Trebbiano grapes and is aged in barrels from a variety of woods. Excellent with all types of greens and vegetables, it is also used for drizzling over fruit (peaches, berries, and melons) and shellfish.

Potato and White Bean Salad

This is delicious as a first course or as a side dish with roast chicken or pork.

Prep time: 25 minutes plus soaking Cook time: 1 hour 20 minutes

    1 cup dry white beans
    2 cups chicken broth, preferably homemade
    2 cups water
    1 yellow onion, peeled
    2 small carrots, peeled and cut in half crosswise
    12 small red new potatoes (about 1¼ pounds), unpeeled
    1 small red onion, quartered and thinly sliced
    1 bunch watercress, rinsed and stemmed
    7 tablespoons extra-virgin olive oil
    2 tablespoons red wine vinegar
    Kosher salt and freshly ground pepper
    2 dozen Niçoise, kalamata, or Gaeta olives

1. Pick over the beans to remove any small stones or debris; rinse thoroughly. Place the beans in a bowl and add cold water to cover by about 2 inches. Soak 6 to 8 hours or overnight. Drain.

2. In a stockpot, combine the beans, broth, water, yellow onion, and carrots; bring to a boil over high heat. Reduce the heat, cover, and simmer, skimming any foam that rises to the surface, 50 to 60 minutes, until the beans are just tender. Be careful not to overcook or boil the beans. Drain and rinse the beans; discarding the onion and carrots. Place the beans in a large bowl.

3. In a large saucepan of boiling salted water, cook the potatoes about 20 minutes, until tender. Drain and let cool. When the potatoes are cool enough to handle, peel and cut them into ¹/₂-inch cubes.

4. Just before serving, add the potatoes to the beans, along with the red onion and watercress; gently toss. Add the olive oil and vinegar and season with salt and pepper. Stir in the olives. Taste and adjust the seasoning and serve immediately.

Makes 6 to 8 servings

Roasted Potato and Garlic Salad with Shallot Vinaigrette

Slow-roasting the potatoes allows them to become a bit crispy on the outside and remain soft on the inside. For maximum flavor, be sure to mix the vinaigrette with the potatoes while they are still warm.

Prep time: 30 minutes Roast time: 1 hour 25 minutes

2 pounds small red potatoes, halved or quartered
8 cloves garlic, peeled
1½ to 2 tablespoons olive oil
Kosher salt

Shallot Vinaigrette:
2 tablespoons champagne or white wine vinegar
1 tablespoon Dijon mustard
⅓ cup extra-virgin olive oil
2 tablespoons finely chopped shallots
Kosher salt and freshly ground black pepper

Chopped fresh flat-leaf parsley, for garnish

1. Preheat the oven to 325° F. Place the potatoes and garlic on a baking sheet. Add the olive oil and salt to taste; toss well to coat. Roast 1¼ to 1½ hours, until the potatoes are fork tender, turning the potatoes and garlic and shaking the pan occasionally.
2. To make the vinaigrette: Whisk the vinegar and mustard together. Slowly add the olive oil in a steady stream, while whisking constantly to emulsify. Whisk in the shallots and salt and pepper to taste. Mix well and let sit for about 20 minutes to blend the flavors.
3. Transfer the warm potatoes and garlic to a large bowl. Drizzle with the vinaigrette and toss well. Taste and adjust the seasonings, garnish with the parsley, and serve.

Makes 6 servings

Summer Tomatoes with Gorgonzola Dressing

Nothing could be more simple or satisfying than a platter of super-fresh, sun-ripened tomatoes doused with a pungent dressing made with Gorgonzola, one of Italy's great cheeses. Serve with crusty baguettes or toasted garlic bread.

Prep time: 10 minutes

> 6 tablespoons extra-virgin olive oil
>
> 2 tablespoons red wine vinegar
>
> Kosher salt and freshly ground black pepper, to taste
>
> 8 ounces Gorgonzola cheese, at room temperature
>
> 6 large ripe tomatoes (about 4 pounds), cored and thickly sliced

1. Combine the olive oil, vinegar, and salt and pepper to taste in a mixing bowl; blend well with a whisk. Add the cheese and gently mash with a fork. The dressing should be slightly lumpy.

2. Just before serving, arrange the tomato slices in an overlapping pattern on a serving dish. Drizzle with the dressing and serve immediately.

Makes 6 to 8 servings

Mixed Cabbage Slaw
with Horseradish Mayonnaise

What would a summer barbecue or picnic be without a big bowl of cole slaw? Try this tangy version which is made with apple cider vinegar and horseradish. It's delicious.

Prep time: 10 minutes plus chilling

> 1 head red cabbage, quartered, cored, and shredded
> 1 head green cabbage, quartered, cored, and shredded
> 3 carrots, peeled and finely shredded
> 1 bunch scallions, finely minced
> 1/2 cup chopped fresh flat-leaf parsley
> 2 cups mayonnaise
> 2 cups plain low-fat yogurt
> 1/4 cup packed light brown sugar
> 2 tablespoons prepared horseradish
> 2 tablespoons apple cider vinegar
> Kosher salt and freshly ground black pepper

1. Place the red and green cabbage, carrots, scallions, and parsley in a large bowl and toss to combine.

2. In a small bowl, whisk the mayonnaise, yogurt, brown sugar, horseradish, and vinegar until well combined. Add salt and pepper; taste and adjust the seasonings and whisk again.

3. Drizzle the dressing over the cabbage mixture and toss thoroughly. Cover and refrigerate the slaw for up to 6 hours before serving.

Makes 10 to 12 servings

Black Bean Salad
with Toasted Cumin Vinaigrette

Bean salad is a nice change of pace from the usual potato and pasta salads that are served all summer. This big-batch, no-fuss salad can be made ahead of time and served chilled or at room temperature.

Prep time: 20 minutes plus soaking the beans and chilling Cook time: 50 minutes

Beans:
4 cups (28 ounces) dried black beans
4 cups chicken broth
4 cups water

1 red bell pepper, stemmed, seeded, deveined, and diced
6 scallions, cut into ½-inch pieces
1 red onion, thinly sliced
¼ cup chopped fresh cilantro
¼ cup chopped fresh flat-leaf parsley
Juice of ½ lemon
Kosher salt and freshly ground black pepper

Toasted Cumin Vinaigrette:
1 tablespoon ground cumin
1 tablespoon chili powder
⅔ cup extra-virgin olive oil
2 tablespoons balsamic vinegar

1. Pick over the beans to remove any small stones or debris; rinse thoroughly. Place the beans in a large bowl and add cold water to cover by about 2 inches. Soak 6 to 8 hours or overnight. Drain.
2. In a stockpot, combine the beans, broth, and water and bring to a boil over high heat. Reduce the heat and simmer uncovered, skimming any foam that rises to the surface, 40 to 50 minutes, until the beans are just tender. Be careful not to overcook or boil the beans. Drain the beans, rinse under cold running water, and set aside to cool.
3. Meanwhile, combine the red pepper, scallions, onion, cilantro, and parsley in a large bowl. Add the lemon juice, season with salt and pepper, and toss gently.

4. To make the vinaigrette: Place the cumin and chili powder in a small skillet and toast over medium heat, stirring constantly, 2 to 3 minutes, just until they begin to smoke. Immediately remove the skillet from the heat. In a small bowl, whisk the olive oil and vinegar together until well combined. Add the toasted spices and whisk again.

5. To assemble the salad, add the cooled beans to the vegetable mixture and toss to mix. Drizzle with the vinaigrette and toss gently. Set aside at room temperature for at least 1 hour to give the flavors time to blend. (Or the salad can be covered and refrigerated for up to 12 hours.) Serve chilled or at room temperature.

Makes 10 to 12 servings

Lentil, Olive, and Feta Salad with Sherry Vinaigrette

For a delicious, Mediterranean-style dinner, serve this salad with Grilled Butterflied Leg of Lamb (page 133) and Cucumber and Mint Salad (page 91). Fabulous.

Prep time: 15 minutes Cook time: 25 minutes

2 tablespoons olive oil
2 cloves garlic, thinly sliced
2½ cups lentils, rinsed
2½ cups water
½ cup kalamata olives, pitted and chopped
½ cup chopped fresh flat-leaf parsley
½ cup (about 2 ounces) crumbled feta cheese
Kosher salt and freshly ground black pepper

Sherry Vinaigrette:
1 tablespoon sherry vinegar
1 tablespoon fresh lemon juice
1 teaspoon Dijon mustard
5 tablespoons extra-virgin olive oil

1. Heat the olive oil in a large skillet or sauté pan over medium-high heat. Add the garlic and cook until softened, about 5 minutes. Add the lentils and stir well to coat. Add the water and bring to a boil. Reduce the heat, cover, and simmer, stirring occasionally, until the lentils are tender and all the liquid is absorbed, about 20 minutes. Drain.
2. In a large bowl, combine the lentils, olives, parsley, one-half of the cheese, and salt and pepper to taste; toss gently to combine.
3. To make the vinaigrette: In a small bowl, whisk together the vinegar, lemon juice, and mustard. Slowly add the extra-virgin olive oil in a steady stream, while whisking constantly to emulsify.
4. Drizzle the vinaigrette over the lentil mixture and toss well to combine. Taste and adjust the seasonings. Sprinkle the salad with the remaining cheese and serve at room temperature.

Makes 8 servings

Warm Fingerling Potato Salad
with Bay Scallops

This is a wonderful salad to make in the fall, when fresh, tender bay scallops become available and fingerling potatoes are at their best.

Prep time: 15 minutes Cook time: 30 minutes

6 fingerling potatoes, rinsed
4 tablespoons olive oil
3/4 pound bay scallops
1 cup cherry or grape tomatoes, halved
1 cup dry white wine
2 shallots, minced
Pinch red pepper flakes
1/4 cup white wine vinegar
1 teaspoon sugar
Kosher salt and freshly ground black pepper
2 bunches watercress, rinsed and stemmed

1. In a pot of boiling salted water, cook the potatoes until fork-tender, about 15 minutes. Drain and keep warm.

2. Heat 2 tablespoons olive oil in a large nonstick skillet. Add the scallops and sauté 1 minute. Stir in the tomatoes and continue cooking until the scallops are cooked through and the tomatoes are warmed, 2 to 3 minutes. Transfer to a large bowl. Slice the potatoes into 1/2-inch pieces and add to the bowl.

3. Return the skillet to the heat and add the wine, shallots, and red pepper flakes. Bring to boil over medium-high heat. Reduce the heat and simmer 2 minutes. Return to a boil and add the vinegar and sugar; stir well. Let the mixture boil until reduced to about 1/3 cup. Remove from the heat, whisk in the remaining 2 tablespoons oil, and season with salt and pepper.

4. Drizzle about one-half of the warm vinaigrette over the scallops, tomatoes, and potatoes in the bowl; toss gently to combine. Arrange the watercress on 6 salad plates. Spoon the scallop mixture on top and drizzle with a bit more vinaigrette, if you like. Season with additional salt and pepper and serve immediately.

Makes 6 servings

Seafood, Green Bean, and Fennel Salad with Fresh Tomato Vinaigrette

This sublime seafood salad is a fabulous entrée. All the ingredients, including the vinaigrette, can be prepared ahead of time and quickly tossed together just before serving.

Prep time: 30 minutes Cook time: 16 minutes

2 (1½-pound) lobsters
1 pound medium shrimp
¾ pound green beans, trimmed
1 small fennel bulb, trimmed, cored, and thinly sliced

Fresh Tomato Vinaigrette:
2 tablespoons extra-virgin olive oil
1 tablespoon champagne or white wine vinegar
Kosher salt and freshly ground black pepper
1 large ripe tomato, cored and finely diced
½ medium red onion, finely diced

1 to 2 tablespoons fresh lemon juice
2 tablespoons fresh basil leaves, thinly sliced
6 cups mixed salad greens
Lemon wedges, for garnish

1. To prepare the lobster: Bring an 8-quart pot three-quarters full of salted water to a vigorous boil. Plunge the lobsters headfirst into the water, cover, and cook over high heat 10 to 12 minutes. Remove the lobsters with tongs; drain and let cool. When cool enough to handle, remove the lobster meat from the tails and claws and cut into bite-sized pieces. Cover and refrigerate.

2. To prepare the shrimp: Bring a large pot of salted water to a vigorous boil. Add the shrimp and simmer until just cooked through, about 3 minutes; drain and let cool. When cool enough to handle, peel and devein. Cover and refrigerate.

3. To prepare the vegetables: Bring a medium pot of salted water to a boil. Add the beans and cook over medium heat until just tender, about 3 minutes. Drain and place in a medium bowl; stir in the fennel. Cover and refrigerate.

4. To prepare the vinaigrette: In a medium bowl, whisk together the olive oil, vinegar, and salt and pepper to taste. Add the tomato (and its juices) and red onion and mix well to combine. Cover and refrigerate.

5. Just before serving, combine the lobster, shrimp, and vegetables in a large bowl. Sprinkle with the lemon juice and basil and toss gently to mix. Drizzle with the vinaigrette and toss again. Taste and adjust the seasonings. Divide the salad greens among 6 plates and spoon the seafood mixture on top. Garnish with lemon wedges and serve immediately.

Makes 6 servings

Grilled Steak Salad with Cherry Tomatoes and Capers

This hearty main-dish salad is especially nice when served with lots of crusty garlic bread and chilled red wine.

Prep time: 50 minutes Grill time: 5 minutes

> 1¼ pounds red and yellow cherry tomatoes,
>   quartered (about 3 cups)
> ½ red onion, minced
> ¼ cup chopped fresh flat-leaf parsley
> 5 tablespoons extra-virgin olive oil
> 2 tablespoons balsamic vinegar
> Kosher salt and freshly ground black pepper
> 2½ to 3 pounds boneless sirloin steaks, about 1 inch thick
> 2 tablespoons fresh lemon juice
> 2 tablespoons drained capers
> 3 cloves garlic, thinly sliced
> 1 bunch arugula, trimmed, rinsed, and dried
> 1 bunch watercress, rinsed and stemmed

1. In a large bowl, combine the tomatoes, onion, parsley, 2 tablespoons olive oil, 1 tablespoon vinegar, and salt and pepper to taste; toss well. Marinate at room temperature 30 minutes.

2. Prepare a medium-hot gas or charcoal grill (coals are covered with a light coating of ash and glow deep red). Grill the steaks, turning, 5 to 7 minutes for medium-rare, or until desired doneness. Let the steaks rest 10 minutes. Cut across the grain into ¼-inch slices.

3. Heat the remaining 3 tablespoons olive oil in a skillet or sauté pan over medium heat. Add the remaining 1 tablespoon vinegar, the lemon juice, capers, and garlic and simmer, stirring frequently, about 5 minutes. In a large bowl, toss together the arugula and watercress. Drizzle the warm dressing over the greens and toss.

4. Arrange the greens on a large platter or individual plates. Top with the steak slices (and their juices). Spoon the tomato mixture on top and serve immediately.

Makes 6 servings

Asian Turkey Salad

One of the best things about cooking Thanksgiving dinner is having lots of luscious leftovers; here's a great way to put that turkey to good use. It's perfect to serve for a light lunch after days of holiday feasting. Feel free to use Chinese, green, or red cabbage (or any combination) instead of the Savoy cabbage.

Prep time: 10 minutes

3 cups shredded cooked turkey
2 cups shredded Savoy cabbage
¼ cup chopped fresh cilantro
2 tablespoons chopped fresh mint leaves
2 scallions, finely minced
1 tablespoon Dijon mustard
1 tablespoon rice vinegar
2 teaspoons soy sauce
1 teaspoon sesame oil
Pinch sugar
¼ cup corn or canola oil
6 cups mixed salad greens

1. Combine the turkey, cabbage, cilantro, mint, and scallions in a large bowl. Toss to mix well.
2. In a small bowl, whisk together the mustard, vinegar, soy sauce, sesame oil, and sugar. Slowly add the oil in a steady stream, whisking constantly to emulsify. Drizzle the vinaigrette over the turkey mixture and toss well to combine.
3. Divide the salad greens among 6 plates. Spoon the turkey salad on top and serve.

Makes 6 servings

Lemon-Grilled Chicken Salad with Haricot Verts and Walnuts

Here's a wonderful main-course salad that's ideal for an informal gathering. Quality walnut oil is well worth seeking out—it adds fantastic flavor.

Prep time: 30 minutes plus marinating Grill time: 35 minutes

Marinade:
Juice of 2 lemons
Juice of 2 limes
2 cloves garlic, thinly sliced
1/4 cup olive oil

3 whole chicken breasts (about 41/2 pounds), split
2 pounds fresh haricots verts or green beans, trimmed

Vinaigrette:
1 tablespoon white wine vinegar
1 teaspoon fresh lemon juice
1/2 cup walnut oil

1/2 cup walnut halves, toasted (page 109)
Kosher salt and freshly ground black pepper

1. To make the marinade: Combine the lemon juice, lime juice, and garlic in a medium bowl. Slowly whisk in the olive oil to combine. Place the chicken in a large nonreactive baking dish. Pour the marinade over the chicken, turning the chicken to coat. Cover and marinate in the refrigerator, turning occasionally, for up to 8 hours or overnight.
2. Prepare a medium-hot gas or charcoal grill (coals are covered with a light coating of ash and glow deep red), or preheat the broiler. Remove the chicken from the marinade, reserving the marinade. Grill or broil the chicken 6 to 9 inches from the heat, turning occasionally, until nicely browned and the juices run clear when the chicken is pierced with a fork, about 30 minutes. Baste the chicken often with the marinade during the first 20 minutes of grilling.
3. Remove the chicken from the heat and set aside to cool. When cool enough to handle, remove the meat from the bones and tear into 11/2-inch pieces. Transfer to a large bowl.

4. In a saucepan of boiling salted water, cook the beans until crisp-tender, 4 to 5 minutes. Rinse under cold running water and drain. Add the beans to the chicken and toss gently.

5. To make the vinaigrette: In a small bowl, whisk together the vinegar and lemon juice. Slowly add the walnut oil in a steady stream, whisking constantly until emulsified.

6. Drizzle about $1/3$ cup vinaigrette over the salad and toss to coat. Heap the salad onto a platter or individual salad plates and sprinkle with the walnut halves. Drizzle with the remaining vinaigrette, season with salt and pepper, and serve immediately.

Makes 6 servings

Toasting Walnuts

To toast the walnuts, spread on a baking sheet and toast in a preheated 350°F oven or toaster oven for about 5 minutes, until golden brown. Shake the pan once or twice for even toasting. Slide the nuts off the baking sheet onto a plate to stop the cooking and let them cool.

Warm Duck Salad with Oranges and Olives

This savory, sumptuous main-course salad combines duck breasts marinated in red wine, oranges, and Niçoise olives for delicious results. Your guests will love it.

Prep time: 20 minutes plus marinating Cook time: 17 minutes

Marinade:
1 cup dry red wine
1 tablespoon light soy sauce
1 tablespoon hot chili sauce with garlic
3 tablespoons chopped orange zest
Juice of 1 orange

2 (1-pound) duck breasts
1 tablespoon olive oil
2 cloves garlic, thinly sliced

Dressing:
¼ cup fresh orange juice
2 tablespoons balsamic vinegar
1 tablespoon Dijon mustard

3 oranges, peeled and cut into bite-sized pieces
½ red onion, thinly sliced
16 Niçoise olives
4 cups mixed salad greens

1. To make the marinade: In a medium bowl, whisk together the wine, soy sauce, chili sauce, orange zest, and orange juice. Place the duck breasts in a large freezer bag or a nonreactive baking dish. Add the marinade and turn the breasts to coat. Seal the bag or cover the dish and marinate in the refrigerator 6 hours or overnight.

2. Heat the olive oil in a large heavy skillet or sauté pan over medium heat. Add the garlic and cook until softened, about 2 minutes. Remove the duck breasts from the marinade and shake off excess liquid; discard the marinade. Add the duck breasts to the pan and cook, turning frequently, until just cooked through, about 15 minutes. Remove the breasts from the pan and let rest on a cutting board about 10 minutes.

3. To make the dressing: Discard the fat from the pan and wipe clean with paper towels. In a small bowl, whisk together the orange juice, vinegar, and mustard until well blended. Add to the pan and cook over medium heat, stirring constantly, until reduced by half, 2 to 3 minutes. Remove from the heat and keep warm.

4. Just before serving, combine the orange pieces, onion, and olives in a bowl. Arrange the greens on a large platter or 6 individual plates. Thinly slice the duck on the diagonal and arrange over the greens. Spoon the orange mixture over the duck. Drizzle with the warm dressing and serve immediately.

Makes 6 servings

Serving Style

Throw an outdoor party in a relaxed atmosphere with a buffet of barbecued chicken from the grill and an array of salads. And don't forget an ice-filled tub of beer and wine!

EASY LIVING

Let your guests lend a hand! Simple tasks such as opening wine and carrying platters outside to the buffet table get everyone involved.

Plates, glasses, and napkins don't always need to match, especially for outdoor parties.

a summer weekend barbecue

Tomatillo Salsa

Zesty Clam Dip

Southern-Style Barbecue Chicken

Black Bean Salad with Toasted Cumin Vinaigrette

Mixed Cabbage Slaw with Horseradish Mayonnaise

Summer Tomatoes with Gorgonzola Dressing

Peach-Berry Cobbler

Cold Beer and Chilled White and Rosé Wine

chapter four

Main Courses

main courses

The dinner table is a symbol of sharing with beloved family and friends, where we celebrate the time-honored tradition of eating a meal together. Without a doubt, there is no better experience than sitting down to a beautifully set table and enjoying a well-cooked meal after hearing the words, "Dinner is served."

Poached Fillet of Beef
with Watercress Sauce

This is a fantastic way to serve fillet of beef for a truly elegant meal. When buying the fillet, have the butcher trim the beef and tie it at 2-inch intervals.

Prep time: 45 minutes   Cook time: 20 minutes

Watercress Sauce:
1 bunch watercress, rinsed and stemmed (about 2½ cups)
½ cup crème fraîche
⅓ cup mayonnaise
1 tablespoon fresh lemon juice
Kosher salt and freshly ground black pepper

Fillet of Beef:
1 (12-inch) piece beef tenderloin, trimmed and tied
4 cups beef broth
4 cups water
1 onion, peeled
1 carrot, peeled and coarsely chopped
2 ribs celery, coarsely chopped
6 sprigs flat-leaf parsley
Kosher salt and freshly ground black pepper

1. To make the sauce: Place the watercress in a food processor and pulse until chopped. Add the crème fraîche, mayonnaise, lemon juice, and salt and pepper and pulse again. Taste and adjust the seasonings. Transfer to a bowl and cover. (The sauce can be refrigerated for up to 3 days; bring to room temperature and stir well before serving.)
2. Cut a piece of cheesecloth large enough to wrap around the fillet twice and to extend about 2 inches beyond each end. Wrap the meat and tie the ends with kitchen string, leaving enough string on each end to lift the fillet from the simmering broth.

3. Combine the broth, water, onion, carrot, celery, parsley, and salt and pepper to taste in a 6-quart stockpot. Bring to a boil. Carefully lower the wrapped fillet into the broth, leaving the strings hanging over the edge of the pot. Reduce the heat to a simmer and poach the meat about 20 minutes, until a meat thermometer inserted in the center registers 120°F. Remove the pot from the heat and carefully lift the fillet from the broth. Let it stand on a cutting board for 15 minutes to cool.

4. Unwrap the fillet and slice into 1/4-inch-thick pieces. Serve warm or at room temperature with the sauce.

Makes 6 to 8 servings

Beef Brisket

Like many good winter foods, this brisket tastes better after a day of slow cooking, so plan accordingly. It is excellent with Vegetable Pancakes (page 168).

Prep time: 30 minutes Bake time: 3 hours, plus reheating

2 tablespoons olive oil

3 medium onions, chopped

3 cloves garlic, thinly sliced

1 (3-pound) first-cut brisket

Kosher salt and freshly ground black pepper

1 (14½- to 16-ounce) can whole plum tomatoes
   with their juice, coarsely chopped

1½ cups dry white wine

2 ribs celery, chopped

1 bay leaf

1 teaspoon chopped fresh rosemary leaves

1 teaspoon chopped fresh oregano

6 carrots, peeled and cut into ½-inch slices

½ cup chopped fresh parsley

1. Preheat the oven to 350° F.

2. Heat 1 tablespoon oil in a large 5- to 6-quart casserole or Dutch oven over medium heat. Add the onions and garlic and cook, stirring, until softened and golden, about 10 minutes. Remove from the heat.

3. Season the brisket generously with salt and pepper. In a large skillet, heat the remaining 1 tablespoon oil over high heat. Add the brisket and cook, turning, until browned, about 4 minutes per side. Lay the brisket in the casserole, fat side up, on top of the onions. Add the tomatoes, wine, celery, bay leaf, rosemary, and oregano.

4. Cover the casserole and bake 2½ hours, basting with the pan juices and turning the meat occasionally. Add the carrots and parsley and continue baking, uncovered, until the carrots are tender, about 30 minutes.

5. Let the brisket cool in the pan, then cover and refrigerate. (The brisket will keep in the refrigerator for up to 2 days.)

6. About 1 hour before serving, preheat the oven to 350° F. Transfer the brisket to a shallow roasting pan or baking dish and spoon the juices and the vegetables on top. Cover tightly with foil and bake until heated through, about 45 minutes. Transfer the brisket to a cutting board and slice across the grain into $1/4$-inch slices.

7. Place the meat and vegetables on a platter, drizzle with the juices, and serve.

Makes 6 servings

Slow-Cooked Beef Stew

There is nothing easier to make—or more delicious to savor—than this beef stew. You simply combine the ingredients in a Dutch oven and slow-cook in the oven for eight hours. It's the perfect dish to come home to after a long, busy day.

Prep time: 10 minutes Bake time: 8 hours

> 2½ pounds beef chuck, cut into 1-inch cubes
> 2 cups dry red wine
> 1 cup beef broth
> 1 cup canned plum tomatoes with juice, coarsely chopped
> 1 cup mushrooms, thinly sliced
> 1 onion, chopped
> 4 carrots, peeled and cut on the diagonal into 1-inch pieces
> 2 parsnips, peeled and cut into 1-inch rounds
> 6 small red new potatoes, halved or quartered
> ¼ cup chopped fresh flat-leaf parsley,
>   plus additional for garnish
> 2 cloves garlic, thinly sliced
> Kosher salt and freshly ground black pepper

1. Preheat the oven to 200° F.
2. Combine the beef, wine, broth, tomatoes, mushrooms, onion, carrots, parsnips, potatoes, parsley, garlic, and salt and pepper to taste in a 3-quart casserole or Dutch oven with a cover. Stir to mix well and cover. Place in the oven and bake 8 hours.
3. Ladle the piping hot stew into shallow soup bowls and garnish with parsley.

Makes 6 servings

Veal Stew with Tomatoes, Peas, and Mushrooms

When making this savory stew, be sure to buy top-quality veal from a butcher.

Prep time: 15 minutes Cook time: 1 hour 45 minutes

> 3 tablespoons olive oil
> 3 tablespoons unsalted butter
> 1/4 cup chopped shallots
> 3 pounds boneless veal, cut into 1 1/2-inch cubes and patted dry
> 2 (28-ounce) cans plum tomatoes, coarsely chopped, with their juice
> Kosher salt and freshly ground black pepper
> 1/2 cup cremini mushrooms, stemmed and thinly sliced
> 1/2 cup stemmed, thinly sliced shiitake mushrooms
> 1 (10-ounce) package frozen peas, thawed
> 1 pound pasta, such as penne or fusilli,
>   cooked according to package instructions (optional)
> 1/2 cup chopped fresh flat-leaf parsley, for garnish

1. In a soup pot or Dutch oven over medium heat, heat 2 tablespoons olive oil and 2 tablespoons butter until the butter melts. Add the shallots and sauté until golden, about 5 minutes. In batches if necessary, add the veal to the pot and cook, turning, until browned well on all sides.

2. Return all the meat to the pot. Add the tomatoes and salt and pepper to taste. Bring to a boil and reduce the heat to a very low simmer. Cook the stew, partially covered and stirring occasionally, until the veal is very tender, about 1 1/2 hours. (At this point, the stew can be cooled, covered, and refrigerated for up to 2 days; bring to room temperature before reheating.)

3. About 20 minutes before serving, heat the remaining 1 tablespoon oil and 1 tablespoon butter in a skillet. Add the cremini and shiitake mushrooms and sauté until nicely browned, about 10 minutes. Stir into the stew. Stir in the peas about 5 minutes before serving. Taste and adjust the seasonings.

4. Serve the stew in shallow bowls over the pasta, if desired. Garnish with parsley.

Makes 6 to 8 servings

Pork, Sweet Potato, and Black Bean Stew

This fabulous one-dish meal is just the thing to serve on a chilly evening.

Prep time: 25 minutes Bake time: 1 hour 35 minutes

> 3½ pounds boneless pork shoulder, cut into 1-inch cubes and patted dry
> Kosher salt and freshly ground black pepper
> 4 tablespoons olive oil
> 2 tablespoons unbleached all-purpose flour
> 1½ cups dry white wine
> 1½ cups chicken broth
> ¼ cup red wine vinegar
> 2 medium sweet potatoes (about 1 pound),
>   peeled and cut into 1-inch cubes
> 1 large onion, coarsely chopped
> 2 cloves garlic, thinly sliced
> ½ cup chopped fresh flat-leaf parsley
> 2 tablespoons ground cumin
> 2 tablespoons Spanish paprika (see below)
> 1 (15-ounce) can black beans, rinsed and drained
> 2 tablespoons fresh lemon juice

1. Preheat the oven to 350° F.
2. Season the pork with salt and pepper. In a soup pot or Dutch oven, heat 2 tablespoons oil over medium-high heat. Add one-half the pork and cook, turning the pieces, until evenly browned. Transfer to a bowl. Repeat with the remaining olive oil and pork.
3. Return all the pork to the pan, sprinkle with flour, and cook over medium heat, tossing well, 3 minutes. Remove from the heat and add the wine, broth, vinegar, sweet potatoes, onion, garlic, ¼ cup parsley, 1 tablespoon cumin, and 1 tablespoon paprika. Mix well and cover. Bake in the oven 1 hour.
4. Add the beans and remaining 1 tablespoon cumin and 1 tablespoon paprika. Stir well, and return to the oven. Bake, uncovered, 20 minutes longer.
5. To serve: Stir in the lemon juice, taste, and adjust the seasonings. Ladle into shallow soup bowls, garnish with the remaining ¼ cup parsley, and serve immediately.

Makes 6 servings

Roasted Pork Loin with Orange-Chile Glaze

Here is a spicy twist on traditional pork roast; it's fabulous with roasted sweet potatoes and grilled vegetables. Ask the butcher to trim the loin and tie it with butcher twine.

Prep time: 30 minutes Roast time: 2 hours

> 1 (4- to 5-pound) center-cut pork loin, trimmed and tied
> Kosher salt and freshly ground black pepper
>
> Orange-Chile Glaze:
> 2 tablespoons chili powder
> 1 tablespoon ground cumin
> 1 tablespoon ground coriander
> 1 1/2 teaspoons ground cinnamon
> 1 cup sugar
> Juice of 2 oranges
> 1/2 cup cider vinegar
> 1/4 cup molasses
> 2 tablespoons finely chopped serrano or poblano chile pepper

1. Preheat the oven to 350° F.
2. Place the pork loin on a rack in a shallow roasting pan and sprinkle lightly with salt and generously with pepper. Roast 1 hour.
3. Meanwhile, to prepare the glaze: In a heavy-bottomed saucepan, combine the chili powder, cumin, coriander, and cinnamon and toast over medium heat, stirring constantly, 2 to 3 minutes, just until the spices begin to smoke and become fragrant. Immediately remove from the heat. Add the sugar, orange juice, vinegar, molasses, and chile; stir well and return to the heat. Bring to a boil, reduce the heat and simmer, stirring occasionally, about 45 minutes, until thickened.
4. After roasting the pork for 1 hour, spoon the pan drippings over the meat and brush generously with the glaze. Insert a meat thermometer into the thickest part of the pork. Roast, occasionally basting with the glaze, 45 to 60 minutes longer, until the thermometer registers 160° F. Let the meat rest 15 minutes. Cut into 1/2-inch-thick slices and serve.

Makes 6 servings

Serving Style

Buffet-style suppers are fun for everyone—including the host. Serve
a delicious make-ahead soup or stew and set up plates or bowls with
napkin-wrapped silverware and let your guests help themselves.

BUFFET STYLE

Mismatched china and stoneware look
so charming and inviting, and they work
well for a buffet-style supper.
Silverware rolled up in napkins is attractive
and convenient. Again, it's all in the mix.

one-dish wonders

Hearty fare, such as Slow-Cooked Beef Stew (page 122), Veal Stew with
Tomatoes, Peas, and Mushrooms (page 123), Pork, Sweet Potato, and Black
Bean Stew (page 124), and Lamb Stew with Garlic-Roasted Potatoes and
Green Beans (page 130) are all excellent choices for one-dish buffet suppers.
All these dishes can (and should) be made ahead of time and served with
nothing more than a salad of mixed greens and lots of crusty bread and red wine.

Baked Ham with Mustard-Rum Glaze

Perfectly baked ham—sweet and deeply browned on the outside and tender and juicy on the inside—is an excellent main course for a large dinner party, a holiday meal, or as part of a buffet. Serve this with a selection of specialty mustards—hot, sweet, and tart. There will be ample leftovers, which are great for sandwiches and salads.

Prep time: 30 minutes Bake time: 1 hour 30 minutes

1 (5-pound) cooked bone-in half ham, excess fat trimmed

Mustard-Rum Glaze:
1 tablespoon Dijon mustard
1 tablespoon dark brown sugar
3 tablespoons dark rum

1. Preheat the oven to 325° F. Line a shallow roasting pan with aluminum foil and set a roasting rack in the pan.
2. Place the ham, fat side up, on the rack. Using a sharp knife, score the fat in a criss-cross or diamond pattern. Insert a meat thermometer into the thickest part of the meat; do not let the thermometer touch the ham bone. Bake about $1^1/2$ hours.
3. To make the glaze: Whisk the mustard and brown sugar together in a small bowl. Stir in the rum, 1 tablespoon at a time, until well blended.
4. About 30 minutes before the ham is done, remove from oven. Brush ham all over with the glaze. Continue baking, basting the ham 2 or 3 times, until it is heated through and the thermometer registers 130° F. Let the ham stand 10 to 15 minutes before carving and serving.

Makes 10 to 12 servings

Lamb Stew with Garlic-Roasted Potatoes and Green Beans

When making stew, you can cook the components separately, as in this flavorful meal.

Prep time: 20 minutes Cook/Roast time: 1 hour 40 minutes

4 to 4½ pounds leg of lamb, boned, trimmed,
    and cut into 1½-inch pieces
Kosher salt and freshly ground black pepper
3 tablespoons olive oil
1 tablespoon unsalted butter
2 medium onions, chopped
12 cloves garlic, 3 thinly sliced, 9 peeled and left whole
1½ cups dry white wine
1 (28-ounce) can plum tomatoes, coarsely chopped,
    with their juice
2 cinnamon sticks
1 tablespoon chopped fresh thyme or 1 teaspoon dried
½ teaspoon ground allspice
1 bay leaf
2 pounds small red new potatoes, halved
1 tablespoon extra-virgin olive oil
1 pound green beans, trimmed
½ cup chopped fresh flat-leaf parsley

1. Season the lamb generously with salt and pepper. In a large soup pot or Dutch oven, heat 2 tablespoons olive oil over medium-high heat. In batches if necessary, add the lamb and cook, turning the pieces, until nicely browned all over, about 5 minutes. Transfer the lamb to a plate; discard any fat left in the pot.

2. Heat the butter and remaining 1 tablespoon olive oil in the pot over medium heat until the butter melts. Add the onions and cook, stirring occasionally, until golden, about 5 minutes. Add the sliced garlic and cook 1 minute longer. Add the wine, tomatoes, cinnamon sticks, thyme, allspice, bay leaf, and salt and pepper to taste and stir well. Return the lamb and its juices to the pot and bring to a boil. Reduce the heat to low, cover, and simmer, stirring occasionally, 1 hour and 15 minutes.

3. Meanwhile, preheat the oven to 350° F. Place the potatoes and whole garlic cloves in a large roasting pan. Drizzle with the extra-virgin olive oil and salt and pepper to taste; toss to coat. Roast the potatoes, stirring occasionally, until lightly browned, about 1 hour.

4. About 10 minutes before serving the lamb, bring a medium saucepan of salted water to a boil. Add the beans and cook over medium-high heat until just tender, about 3 minutes; drain.

5. Just before serving, stir the beans into the stew. Divide the potatoes among 6 or 8 shallow soup bowls and spoon the stew on top. Garnish with parsley and serve immediately.

Makes 6 to 8 servings

Grilled Sirloin Steak with Chimichurri Sauce

Chimichurri sauce, a piquant blend of fresh parsley, garlic, olive oil, and vinegar, is an indispensable condiment. Not only is it fabulous with grilled steak but it is also very good as a dip with bread and vegetables or for drizzling over a salad.

Prep time: 25 minutes Grill time: 10 minutes

Chimichurri Sauce:
1 cup fresh flat-leaf parsley, coarsely chopped
5 cloves garlic, peeled
½ cup extra-virgin olive oil
2 tablespoons red wine vinegar
Pinch red pepper flakes
Kosher salt and freshly ground black pepper

3 pounds boneless sirloin steak

1. To make the sauce: Place the parsley and garlic in a food processor and pulse until blended. Slowly add the olive oil through the feed tube. Add the vinegar, red pepper flakes, and salt and pepper to taste; pulse until well blended. Cover and refrigerate until ready to serve (or for up to 2 days). Bring to room temperature before serving.
2. Season the steak generously with salt and pepper. Prepare a medium-hot gas or charcoal grill (coals are covered with a light coating of ash and glow deep red). Grill the steaks, turning, 10 to 15 minutes for medium-rare. Transfer to a cutting board and let rest 10 minutes. Slice the steaks against the grain into 1/4-inch slices. Serve with the sauce.

Makes 6 servings

Grilled Butterflied Leg of Lamb

A marinade of balsamic vinegar and red wine flavored with fresh garden herbs gives this grilled lamb a wonderful aroma.

Prep time: 20 minutes plus marinating Grill time: 30 minutes

> 1 cup dry red wine
> ¼ cup balsamic vinegar
> ¼ cup olive oil
> 4 large cloves garlic, thinly sliced
> ¼ cup chopped fresh mint
> 1 tablespoon crushed fresh rosemary
> 1 teaspoon chopped fresh oregano
> Freshly ground black pepper
> 1 (4- to 5-pound) butterflied leg of lamb (see below)

1. In a small bowl, combine the wine, vinegar, olive oil, garlic, mint, rosemary, oregano, and pepper to taste; whisk to mix. Place the lamb in a large shallow glass or ceramic baking dish and pour the marinade over it. Cover and marinate in the refrigerator, turning the lamb occasionally, about 6 hours.
2. Prepare a medium-hot gas or charcoal grill (coals are covered with white ash and glow deep red).
3. Remove the lamb from the marinade, letting the excess drip off. Transfer the reserved marinade to a small saucepan and bring to a boil over medium-high heat. Boil 2 minutes.
4. Grill the lamb 4 to 6 inches from the heat, turning once and basting frequently with the boiled marinade, 30 to 40 minutes. After 30 minutes, check the lamb every few minutes—when it's done it should be medium-rare, still red in the center; do not overcook. Carve the lamb into thin slices and serve immediately.

Makes 6 to 8 servings

Buying Butterflied Leg of Lamb
Butterflied leg of lamb is a leg with the bone removed so that the meat can be laid flat for grilling or broiling. When buying the lamb, remind the butcher that the weight refers to the amount of meat needed after the bone has been removed.

Grilled Pork and Pineapple Kabobs

The combination of grilled pork and pineapple is irresistible. These simple kabobs are great served with grilled scallions, although grilled red or yellow peppers would be delicious, too.

Prep time: 25 minutes Grill time: 15 minutes

Marinade:

1½ cups pineapple juice

Juice of 3 limes

3 tablespoons olive oil

3 tablespoons brown sugar

3 to 4 scallions, roughly chopped

2½ pounds trimmed boned pork loin or butt,
   cut into 1½-inch cubes

1 (3¾- to 4¼-pound) fresh pineapple

12 large scallions, trimmed

Olive oil for brushing

1.   To make the marinade: In a large nonreactive bowl, combine the pineapple juice, lime juice, olive oil, and brown sugar. Add the chopped scallions and stir to mix. Add the pork and toss to coat. Cover and marinate in the refrigerator, stirring several times, at least 4 or up to 12 hours.

2.   Trim the leaves off the pineapple. Hold the pineapple upright on a cutting board and slice the skin off the fruit. Slice the peeled fruit in half and cut out the core. Cut the fruit into $1^1/2$- to 2-inch chunks. You will have about 18 cubes or 4 cups.

3.   Prepare a medium-hot gas or charcoal grill (coals are covered with a light coating of ash and glow deep red). Spray the grill rack with vegetable oil spray.

4.   Thread about 6 cubes of pork and 3 chunks of pineapple on each of six 12-inch skewers, beginning and ending with pork and interspersing the pineapple. Discard the marinade.

5.   Grill the kabobs, turning several times, 12 to 15 minutes, until the pork is cooked through and the pineapple is lightly charred. The pork is done when an instant-read thermometer inserted into a cube registers 155° F or slightly higher.

6.   Meanwhile, brush the scallions lightly with oil and lay on the outer edges of the grill. Grill, turning with tongs, about 5 minutes, until charred.

7.   Remove the pork and pineapple from the skewers and serve with the scallions.

Makes 6 servings

Herb-Roasted Chicken

What is better than a simple roasted chicken? Two of them! Two are just as easy to roast as one and they're always delicious.

Prep time: 20 minutes Roast time: 1 hour 20 minutes

> 2 (4-pound) chickens, rinsed and patted dry
> 1 medium yellow onion, peeled and cut into large chunks
> 1 medium lemon, quartered
> 4 sprigs fresh tarragon
> 2 sprigs fresh rosemary
> 1 tablespoon unsalted butter, at room temperature
> Kosher salt and freshly ground black pepper

1. Preheat the oven to 425° F.
2. Place the chickens on a rack in a large roasting pan. Stuff the cavities with the onion, lemon, tarragon, and rosemary. Truss with kitchen string. Rub the butter all over the skin of both chickens and season generously with salt and pepper.
3. Roast the chickens 15 minutes. Turn the oven dial down to 375° F and continue roasting until the juices run clear when the thigh is pierced with a fork, about 1 hour and 20 minutes. Remove from the oven and let cool slightly, about 10 minutes, before carving. Serve warm or at room temperature, or refrigerate the chicken before carving and serve cold.

Makes 8 servings

Coq au Vin with Pearl Onions and Wild Mushrooms

This classic French chicken dish is great for winter dinner parties, especially since it can (and should) be made a day ahead of time to let the flavors of the chicken, wine, and vegetables marinate and intensify. Serve with lots of crusty French bread, followed by a salad and cheese.

Prep time: 45 minutes plus chilling Bake time: 2 hours 30 minutes

6 slices bacon, diced

2 tablespoons unsalted butter

2 (2½- to 3-pound) chickens, each cut into 10 pieces

16 pearl onions, peeled

4 scallions, minced

8 cloves garlic, peeled

1 pound cremini mushrooms, wiped clean and quartered

1 tablespoon unbleached all-purpose flour

1 (750-ml) bottle dry red wine

1 cup chicken broth

1 tablespoon chopped fresh thyme or 1 teaspoon dried

Kosher salt and freshly ground black pepper

16 small red potatoes

6 ounces fresh wild mushrooms (such as shiitakes or chanterelles),
  thinly sliced

½ cup chopped fresh flat-leaf parsley, for garnish

1. One day before serving: Fry the bacon in a large Dutch oven until crisp. Transfer with a slotted spoon to paper towels to drain; set aside. Add 1 tablespoon butter to the drippings in the pan. In batches if necessary, add the chicken and cook, turning, until lightly browned. Transfer the chicken to a large bowl and set aside.

2. Add the onions, scallions, and garlic to the pan and sauté over medium heat 5 minutes. Add the cremini mushrooms and sauté 5 minutes longer. Sprinkle the flour over the vegetables and cook, 1 minute, stirring to coat the vegetables. Add the wine and broth, stirring constantly. Season with thyme and salt and pepper. Bring to a boil and remove from the heat. Add the reserved bacon and chicken, and the potatoes; stir well. Cover and refrigerate overnight.

3. The next day, let the coq au vin come to room temperature. Preheat the oven to 350° F.

4. Heat the remaining 1 tablespoon butter in a skillet over medium-high heat. Add the wild mushrooms and sauté until browned, about 10 minutes. Set aside.

5. Bake the coq au vin, covered, in the oven for 1 hour. Add the wild mushrooms and stir well. Bake 40 minutes longer, until the juices run clear when the chicken is pierced with a fork and the meat is falling off the bone. Serve the coq au vin in large shallow bowls garnished with parsley.

Makes 8 servings

Southern-Style Barbecue Chicken

Barbecued chicken is a summertime tradition all across the country. The secret of this variation of an old Southern recipe is to first marinate the chicken overnight in a brew of vinegar and spicy whole cloves, then baste with the barbecue sauce during the last half of cooking time. Be sure to grill the chicken over slow-burning coals; they should be covered with white ash before putting the chicken pieces on the grill. Otherwise, the chicken will cook too fast.

Prep time: 15 minutes plus marinating Grill time: 30 minutes

4 cups water

2 1/2 cups white vinegar

12 whole cloves

Kosher salt and freshly ground black pepper

2 (2 1/2- to 3-pound) frying chickens, cut into 10 pieces each
(breast cut into 4 pieces)

Barbecue Sauce:

2 tablespoons corn oil

1/3 cup sliced yellow onion (about 1 small onion)

2 cloves garlic, thinly sliced

1 1/2 cups tomato ketchup

1/2 cup packed brown sugar

Juice of 1/2 lemon

2 tablespoons Worcestershire sauce

2 teaspoons chili powder

1 teaspoon Dijon mustard

1 teaspoon hot sauce

1. The day before serving, combine the water, vinegar, cloves, and salt and pepper to taste in a shallow glass or ceramic bowl. Add the chicken pieces and turn several times to coat. Cover and marinate in the refrigerator, turning occasionally, overnight.

2. To make the barbecue sauce: Heat the oil in a large skillet over medium-high heat. Add the onion and garlic and cook about 5 minutes, until golden; do not burn the garlic. Add the ketchup, brown sugar, lemon juice, Worcestershire sauce, chili powder, mustard, and hot sauce. Stir constantly until the sauce comes to a simmer. Reduce the heat to low and simmer, stirring occasionally, 45 to 60 minutes, until the sauce is reduced and thickened. Remove from the heat and let cool. Reserve 1 cup of the sauce to serve with the chicken.

3. Prepare a low gas or charcoal grill (the coals are covered with white ash). Remove the chicken from the marinade; discard the marinade. Grill the chicken about 15 minutes, turning frequently for even cooking. Continue cooking, basting with the remaining sauce, 15 to 25 minutes longer, until the juices run clear when the chicken is pierced with a fork. Serve the chicken with the reserved barbecue sauce.

Makes 6 to 8 servings

Citrus-Grilled Game Hens

Cornish game hens bathed in a marinade of lime and orange juice, garlic, and olive oil, are a natural for grilling. They're delicious served hot, cold, or at room temperature.

Prep time: 15 minutes plus marinating Bake/Grill time: 30 minutes

> 6 (1¼-pound) Cornish game hens, halved
> 1 cup fresh lime juice (from about 1½ pounds limes)
> ½ cup orange juice
> 2 tablespoons olive oil
> 3 cloves garlic, thinly sliced
> Kosher salt and freshly ground black pepper
> 2 bunches fresh watercress, rinsed and stemmed

1.   Place the hens in a large, shallow glass or ceramic bowl. In a small bowl, whisk the lime juice, orange juice, oil, garlic, and salt and pepper to taste. Pour the marinade over the hens and turn to coat thoroughly. Cover and marinate in the refrigerator, turning occasionally, 4 to 6 hours.

2.   Preheat the oven to 350° F. Prepare a medium-hot gas or charcoal grill (coals are covered with a light coating of ash and glow deep red).

3.   Transfer the hens and one-half the marinade to a shallow baking pan; reserving the remaining marinade. Bake the hens 20 minutes.

4.   Meanwhile, transfer the reserved marinade to a small saucepan and bring to a boil over medium-high heat. Boil 2 minutes. Set aside.

5.   Remove the hens from the oven; discard the marinade in the pan. Grill the hens, basting often with the reserved boiled marinade, 10 minutes on each side, until nicely browned and the juices run clear when a thigh is pierced with a fork. Place the watercress on a large platter, place the hens on top, and serve immediately.

Makes 6 servings

Red Snapper
with Creamy Tomato-Basil Sauce

Slow-cooked red snapper, a mild and fairly sweet-tasting fish, is especially delicious topped with a light cream sauce, made with fresh ripe tomatoes and basil. You can also use other types of snapper, or sole or orange roughy.

Prep time: 15 minutes Cook time: 16 minutes

 3 tablespoons olive oil
 6 ($1/2$-pound) skinless red snapper fillets
 Kosher salt and freshly ground black pepper
 2 small cloves garlic, thinly sliced
 $1^{1}/_{2}$ cups chopped ripe tomato (about 1 pound)
 3 tablespoons chopped fresh basil
 3 to 4 tablespoons heavy cream

1. Place $1^{1}/_{2}$ tablespoons olive oil in a large nonstick skillet and add the fillets, skinned side down; turn to coat with the oil. Season with salt and pepper. Cover and cook the fish over low heat until just cooked through, about 10 to 15 minutes. Transfer the fillets to a platter, cover with foil, and set aside.

2. Heat the remaining $1^{1}/_{2}$ tablespoons oil in the skillet over medium heat. Add the garlic and sauté until softened, about 2 minutes. Add the tomatoes and cook 1 minute. Stir in 2 tablespoons basil and cook 1 minute. Stir in the cream and cook until just warmed through, about 2 minutes longer. Pour the tomato-cream sauce over the fish, garnish with the remaining 1 tablespoon basil, and serve immediately.

Makes 6 servings

Spicy Shrimp and Bell Pepper Creole

Shrimp Creole is traditionally made with green peppers, but this recipe uses sweeter red and yellow peppers which complement the shrimp perfectly.

Prep time: 10 minutes Cook time: 45 minutes

2 tablespoons olive oil

1 medium onion, finely chopped

3 cloves garlic, thinly sliced

1 red bell pepper, seeded, deveined, and diced

1 yellow bell pepper, seeded, deveined, and diced

1 rib celery, thinly sliced

Pinch red pepper flakes

Pinch cayenne pepper

4 medium ripe tomatoes, coarsely chopped, or 1 (28-ounce) can
  plum tomatoes, coarsely chopped with their juice

1 cup clam juice

1 cup low-fat chicken broth

1 teaspoon chopped fresh thyme, or 1/2 teaspoon dried

Kosher salt and freshly ground black pepper

2 pounds shrimp, peeled and deveined

Dash hot sauce

3 cups cooked basmati or yellow rice, for serving

1/4 cup chopped fresh flat-leaf parsley, for garnish

1. In a large soup pot or Dutch oven, heat the oil over medium heat. Add the onion and garlic and cook until golden, about 5 minutes. Add the red and yellow peppers, celery, red pepper flakes, and cayenne and cook, stirring occasionally, 5 minutes. Add the tomatoes, clam juice, broth, thyme, and salt and pepper to taste. Bring to a boil, reduce the heat, and cover. Simmer over low heat, stirring occasionally, 25 to 30 minutes. (The dish can be prepared up to this point, covered, and refrigerated for up to 2 days.)

2. Add the shrimp and hot sauce to the tomato mixture; cook, stirring occasionally, until the shrimp turn pink and are cooked through, 5 to 7 minutes. Serve over rice in large shallow bowls, garnished with parsley.

Makes 6 servings

Mussels Provençale

This classic dish is so easy to prepare and can be made just about any time of year. When fresh tomatoes are not available, use fine canned plum tomatoes, such as San Marzano. Serve in oversized soup bowls along with lots of crusty bread for dipping.

Prep time: 10 minutes Cook time: 13 minutes

¼ cup olive oil
1 small onion, thinly sliced
4 cloves garlic, thinly sliced
1 cup dry white wine
7 ripe fresh plum tomatoes, chopped, or 1 (28-ounce) can plum tomatoes, chopped, with their juice
3 pounds fresh mussels, scrubbed, debearded, and rinsed
½ cup chopped fresh parsley
2 tablespoons thinly sliced basil leaves

Heat the oil in a large saucepan or stockpot over medium heat. Add the onion and garlic and sauté until softened, about 5 minutes. Add the wine and tomatoes, cover, and bring to a boil over high heat. Add the mussels, parsley, and basil. Cover, reduce the heat to medium-high, and cook about 5 minutes, until the mussels open. Discard any that do not open. Spoon the mussels and tomato broth into shallow bowls and serve piping hot.

Makes 6 servings

Grilled Salmon Fillet
with Herbed Yogurt Sauce

Grilled salmon has a wonderful taste and pairs well with many side dishes. Feel free to use other types of herbs in the sauce: tarragon, basil, and chives all work well.

Prep time: 15 minutes Grill time: 5 minutes

1 center-cut salmon fillet (about 3 pounds), patted dry
1 tablespoon olive oil
1 teaspoon fresh lemon juice
Kosher salt and freshly ground black pepper

Herbed Yogurt Sauce:
1 cup plain yogurt
1 tablespoon chopped fresh flat-leaf parsley
1 tablespoon chopped fresh dill
1 tablespoon chopped fresh mint
Freshly ground black pepper

Lemon wedges, for serving

1. Prepare a medium gas or charcoal grill (coals are covered with a light coating of ash and glow deep red). Spray a seafood grilling rack with vegetable oil spray.
2. Brush the fish lightly with the oil and lemon juice and season with salt and pepper. Place the salmon, skin side down, in the prepared grilling rack. Place the rack on the grill. Grill the salmon, covered, until cooked throughout, 5 to 7 minutes. Transfer the salmon to a cutting board and let sit 2 to 3 minutes.
3. To make the yogurt sauce: In a small bowl, combine the yogurt, parsley, dill, mint, and pepper. Taste and adjust the seasonings.
4. With a very sharp knife, cut the salmon into 6 equal pieces. Serve with the yogurt sauce and lemon wedges.

Makes 6 servings

Spaghetti and Manila Clam Sauce

Pasta with clam sauce is a great dish for a casual dinner because it's so quick and easy. It is delicious made it with small, sweet-tasting Manila clams, but it works well with littlenecks as well. Be sure to toss the pasta with the sauce in the pot before serving, so each strand of spaghetti is coated with the sauce.

Prep time: 25 minutes Cook time: 30 minutes

> 1 pound spaghetti
> 3 slices bacon
> 2 tablespoons olive oil
> 1 small onion, finely chopped
> 2 cloves garlic, thinly sliced
> 1½ to 2 pounds Manila or littleneck clams
> 1 cup dry white wine
> Pinch red pepper flakes
> ½ cup chopped fresh flat-leaf parsley
> Freshly ground black pepper to taste

1. Bring a large pot of salted water to a boil. Add the spaghetti and cook according to package directions until al dente.
2. Meanwhile, cook the bacon in a large skillet or sauté pan, turning, until crisp. Transfer to paper towels to drain. When cool enough to handle, crumble the bacon; set aside.
3. Add the olive oil to the bacon drippings and heat over medium heat. Add the onion and garlic and cook, stirring, until softened and golden, about 7 minutes. Add the clams, wine, and red pepper flakes. Cover and cook over high heat until the clams open, 3 to 5 minutes. Discard any clams that do not open.
4. Drain the pasta and return to the pot. Add the clam sauce, parsley, and reserved bacon and toss well. Season with pepper and serve immediately.

Makes 4 servings

Wild Mushroom Lasagna

Here's an elegant lasagna, made special with porcini mushrooms and creamy béchamel. The mushroom-tomato sauce can be made a few days ahead, so the dish isn't too labor-intensive. This is wonderful, so enjoy!

Prep time: 50 minutes Bake time: 1 hour 30 minutes

Mushroom-Tomato Sauce:
1 cup (4 ounces) dried porcini mushrooms
2 cups boiling water
3 tablespoons olive oil
3 ounces shiitake mushrooms, stemmed and thinly sliced
3 ounces cremini mushrooms, stemmed and thinly sliced
1 cup chopped onion
1 (28-ounce) can diced tomatoes
2 tablespoons chopped fresh basil
Pinch sugar
Kosher salt and freshly ground black pepper

Béchamel:
3 tablespoons unsalted butter
2½ tablespoons unbleached all-purpose flour
3 cups whole milk, heated
Pinch kosher salt and freshly ground black pepper

12 ruffle-edged dried lasagna noodles (do not use no-boil noodles)
1¾ cups (about 7 ounces) finely grated Parmesan cheese

1. To make the mushroom-tomato sauce: Place the porcini mushrooms in a medium bowl, add the boiling water, and let stand until softened, about 20 minutes. Lift out the porcini, squeeze the excess liquid back into the bowl, and rinse to remove any grit. Strain the soaking liquid through a sieve lined with a paper towel into another bowl; set aside. Chop the porcini mushrooms; set aside.

2. Meanwhile, heat 1 tablespoon oil in a large heavy skillet over medium heat. Add the shiitake and cremini mushrooms and sauté until nicely browned, 5 to 7 minutes. Transfer to a bowl and set aside.

3. Wipe out the skillet. Heat the remaining 2 tablespoons oil in the skillet over medium heat. Add the onion and cook, stirring occasionally, until softened, about 5 minutes. Stir in the tomatoes with their juice, the reserved sautéed mushrooms, the reserved porcini mushrooms, and $1^1/_2$ cups of the soaking liquid. Simmer the sauce, stirring frequently, until thickened, 15 to 20 minutes. Stir in the basil, sugar, and salt and pepper to taste; simmer 10 minutes. Add a bit more of the porcini liquid if the sauce seems too thick. (The sauce can be cooled, covered, and refrigerated for up to 2 days; bring to room temperature before proceeding.)

4. To make the béchamel: Melt the butter in a heavy saucepan over medium-low heat. Add the flour and cook over low heat, whisking constantly, 3 minutes. Add the warm milk in a slow, steady stream, whisking vigorously, until well-combined. Add salt to taste. Bring to a boil, add pepper to taste, and whisk until thickened, about 10 minutes. Set aside.

5. To cook the noodles: Bring a large pot of salted water to a boil. Add the lasagna noodles and cook according to package directions until al dente, about 8 minutes. Drain and transfer to a bowl of cold water. When cool, lay the noodles on a kitchen towel and pat dry.

6. To assemble the lasagna: Preheat the oven to 425° F and set the oven rack in the middle position. Butter the bottom of a 9 x 13-inch baking dish; spread with 1 cup béchamel. Arrange 3 lasagna noodles over the sauce. Top with one-third of the tomato sauce and spread evenly. Sprinkle with $1/_3$ cup cheese. Repeat the layering of pasta, tomato sauce, and cheese twice. Cover with the last 3 lasagna noodles. Spread the remaining béchamel on top and sprinkle with the remaining $3/_4$ cup cheese.

7. Bake the lasagna, uncovered, until it is bubbling and the top is browned, 30 to 35 minutes. Let stand at room temperature at least 15 minutes before cutting.

Makes 6 to 8 servings

Risotto with Red Wine and Mushrooms

Risotto is a good dish if you like to entertain informally in the kitchen. Because the rice needs diligent attention, it is best if the cook has friends to talk to and share a glass of wine with while stirring—or better yet, to pitch in and help! Be sure to have all the ingredients ready before you start so that you can devote your time and attention to the rice, which requires at least 15 minutes at the stove.

Prep time: 45 minutes Cook time: 60 minutes

> 1 cup (4 ounces) dried porcini mushrooms
> 1 cup boiling water
> 3 tablespoons olive oil
> 1 pound portobello mushrooms (about 4 large), stemmed and sliced
> 2 cloves garlic, sliced
> 1/2 cup chopped flat-leaf parsley
> 2 tablespoons fresh lemon juice
> Kosher salt and freshly ground black pepper
> 1 quart chicken broth, preferably homemade
> 5 tablespoons unsalted butter
> 1 red onion, diced
> 1 1/2 cups uncooked Arborio rice
> 1/2 cup dry red wine
> 1/2 cup freshly grated Parmesan cheese, plus more for garnish

1. Place the porcini mushrooms in a medium bowl, add the water, and let stand until softened, about 20 minutes. Lift out the porcini, squeeze the excess liquid back into the bowl, and rinse to remove any grit; set aside. Strain the soaking liquid through a sieve lined with a paper towel into another bowl; set aside.

2. Heat the olive oil in a large sauté pan over medium heat. Add the portobello mushrooms and sauté about 15 minutes, until they begin to soften. Add the garlic and porcini mushrooms and cook 3 to 4 minutes, until the garlic is softened. Add one-half the soaking liquid and cook about 10 minutes, until the liquid is reduced to about 1 tablespoon. Stir in the parsley and lemon juice and season with salt and pepper. Set aside, covered, to keep warm. (If the lid is not tight fitting or the kitchen is drafty, transfer to a 200° F oven to keep warm.)

3.   In a saucepan, bring the broth to a boil over high heat. Reduce the heat and simmer while making the risotto.

4.   In a large saucepan or stockpot, melt 4 tablespoons butter over medium heat. Add the onion and sauté about 5 minutes, just until softened. Remove the pan from the heat and add the rice, stirring until coated with butter. Return to the heat and stir in the remaining mushroom soaking liquid. Add 2 ladlefuls of hot broth (about $1/2$ cup), stirring constantly, until the rice absorbs nearly all the liquid. Continue stirring and adding more simmering broth, a ladleful or two at a time, and not adding more broth until the previous amount is absorbed by the rice. When nearly all the broth has been added, the risotto will be creamy but the individual grains will be slightly firm (al dente). When the risotto reaches this point, stop adding broth.

5.   Add the remaining 1 tablespoon butter and the wine, stirring until both are well absorbed. Add the warm mushroom mixture and the Parmesan and stir gently, being careful not to overmix. Serve immediately in large pasta or soup bowls with additional Parmesan cheese grated over the top.

Makes 6 servings

Serving Style

Simple white china, candles, and flowers add a touch of elegance to the dining room and dinner table.

IT'S IN THE MIX

Don't be afraid to mix and match candle sticks and candle colors—but keep the flower arrangements simple.

A PROPER PLACE SETTING

When setting the table, keep in mind these basic placements: Napkins and forks are placed on the left of the plate, knives and spoons are on the right—with the blade of the knife facing toward the plate. A teaspoon for coffee or dessert is sometimes set at the top.

UNDERSTATED ELEGANCE

Plain white candles on glass pedestals add a beautiful glow to the dining room. Note that candles for the table and dining room should always be unscented.

Bunches of white tulips set in varied wine goblets add simple elegance to the table.

chapter five

Side Dishes

side dishes

Side dishes—important and special components of every meal—should feature the freshest vegetables (sautéed, slow-roasted, or grilled) as well as beans, rice, or grains that complement the main course deliciously. And don't forget the homemade breads, biscuits, and relishes; they are well worth the effort and will surely delight your guests.

Asparagus with Fresh Chives and Mint

Asparagus is an elegant vegetable that is especially plentiful and flavorful in the spring, its natural growing season. Indulge in it as often as possible, serving it with little embellishment alongside other springtime foods, such as salmon and lamb. Look for straight stalks with tightly closed and pointed tips.

Prep time: 15 minutes Cook time: 10 minutes

> 3 pounds slender fresh asparagus
> 4 tablespoons (½ stick) unsalted butter
> 2 tablespoons finely chopped shallots
> 1 teaspoon finely grated lemon zest
> 1 tablespoon fresh lemon juice
> Kosher salt
> 3 tablespoons finely snipped fresh chives
> 2 teaspoons finely chopped fresh mint leaves
> Freshly ground black pepper

1. Cut or break off the tough woody ends of the asparagus stalks and discard (young asparagus may not have tough ends). Using a vegetable peeler and starting just below the tip, peel the skin from each stalk.
2. In a large saucepan or skillet of lightly salted boiling water, cook the asparagus 3 to 5 minutes, just until tender. Drain well.
3. In a saucepan over medium heat, melt 1 tablespoon butter. Add the shallots and cook, stirring, 2 to 3 minutes, until transparent and softened. Add the remaining 3 tablespoons butter and continue stirring until the butter melts. Remove from the heat and stir in the lemon zest, lemon juice, and 1 teaspoon salt. Stir in the chives and mint.
4. In a shallow bowl, combine the asparagus and butter mixture and carefully toss. Season with additional salt and pepper and serve immediately.

Makes 6 servings

Baby Bok Choy and Shiitake Mushrooms

Bok choy, a mild-tasting and versatile vegetable, pairs very nicely with shiitake mushrooms. Baby bok choy is more tender, but if you cannot find it, it's fine to use regular bok choy. Be sure to have all your ingredients ready before starting this quick stir-fry.

Prep time: 10 minutes Cook time: 9 minutes

1/2 cup chicken broth

2 tablespoons Asian fish sauce

1 teaspoon soy sauce

2 tablespoons canola oil

2 cloves garlic, thinly sliced

2 tablespoons minced fresh ginger

1 cup stemmed, thinly sliced shiitake mushrooms

2 pounds baby bok choy (leaves and stems),
   cut into 1-inch pieces

1. In a small bowl, whisk together the broth, fish sauce, and soy sauce; set aside.

2. In a large skillet or wok over high heat, heat the oil until very hot. Add the garlic and ginger and stir-fry about 30 seconds, until fragrant. Add the mushrooms and stir-fry 2 minutes. Add the bok choy and stir-fry until crisp-tender, about 3 minutes.

3. Add the broth mixture and cook until the bok choy is tender but still bright green and the sauce is slightly reduced, about 3 minutes longer. Serve immediately.

Makes 6 servings

Sautéed Kale, Spinach, and Collard Greens

Fresh greens are simple to prepare, requiring only a large pan and a few minutes over good heat to wilt, release their liquid, and turn a gorgeous dark green. If you have a pan that is large enough, cook all the greens at once; if not, cook them in two or three batches. Keep in mind that fresh greens shrink considerably when cooked, so the mass you begin with may seem overly large. It isn't.

Prep time: 10 minutes Cook time: 6 minutes per batch

> 2 tablespoons olive oil, plus more if necessary
> 2 (1-pound) bunches spinach, washed well and stemmed
> 2 (1-pound) bunches collard greens, washed well and stemmed
> 1 (1-pound) bunch green or purple kale, washed well and stemmed
> Kosher salt and freshly ground black pepper

1.   In a large skillet, heat the oil over medium-high heat. Add as much spinach, collards and kale as will fit in the pan and cook, stirring, about 5 minutes, until the greens begin to wilt. Season with salt and pepper. With tongs, transfer the greens to a large bowl. Continue cooking the remaining greens, adding more oil to the pan if necessary and transferring each cooked batch to the bowl. When all the greens are wilted, return them to the pan and stir to mix.

2.   Cover the pan and steam the greens over medium-high heat for about 1 minute. Uncover and cook for a few minutes longer, until any liquid evaporates. Taste, adjust the seasonings, toss, and serve immediately.

Makes 6 to 8 servings

Washing Greens
The trickiest part of cooking greens is washing them well. Fill a sink with cold water and soak the greens for several minutes, gently swirling them to remove all grit and sand. Rinse in a colander under gently running cold water and then break off the tough stems. There is no need to drain the greens once washed; just give them a good shake.

Corn and Carrot Pudding

Grated carrots and fresh rosemary add savory flavor to this delicious corn pudding, an ideal dish to serve alongside baked ham or a pork roast.

Prep time: 10 minutes   Bake time: 50 minutes

> 2 carrots, finely grated
> 3 large eggs, lightly beaten
> 1 cup milk
> 1 cup heavy cream
> 4 tablespoons (1/2 stick) unsalted butter, melted
> 1 tablespoon unbleached all-purpose flour
> 1 tablespoon sugar
> Kosher salt and freshly ground black pepper
> 2 cups fresh or frozen corn kernels (see below)
> 1 tablespoon chopped fresh rosemary

1. Preheat the oven to 325° F. Butter an 11 x 6 x 2-inch baking dish.
2. In a large bowl, combine the carrots, eggs, milk, cream, butter, flour, and sugar and stir to mix. Season with salt and pepper. Gently stir in the corn and rosemary.
3. Transfer the mixture to the prepared baking dish and set the dish in a larger roasting pan. Place the pan in the oven and add enough boiling water to come halfway up the sides of the smaller dish. Bake 50 to 60 minutes, until browned and a knife inserted in the center comes out clean. Let the pudding stand 10 to 15 minutes before serving.

Makes 6 to 8 servings

Using Fresh Corn

If at all possible, use fresh corn in this dish for the best flavor. For 2 cups fresh corn kernels, use 3 or 4 ears of corn, depending on their size. Shuck the ears and cook in boiling water 3 to 4 minutes. When cool, scrape the kernels from the ears with a sharp knife. (If using frozen corn, there is no need to cook the kernels.)

Spiced Baby Carrots
with Moroccan Olives

Strong-tasting, salty Moroccan olives are the perfect foil for sweet baby carrots.

Prep time: 15 minutes plus marinating Cook time: 3 minutes

> 4 dozen baby carrots, with some stem attached, peeled
>   and halved lengthwise, or 2 dozen mature carrots,
>   with some stem attached, peeled and cut lengthwise
>   and crosswise into 2-inch-long pieces
> Pinch kosher salt
> 1/2 cup extra-virgin olive oil
> 1 tablespoon fresh lemon juice
> 1/2 teaspoon ground cumin
> 1/2 teaspoon paprika
> 1/4 teaspoon ground cinnamon
> Pinch cayenne pepper
> 1/4 cup pitted, halved Moroccan olives, or other cured,
>   salty black olives such as kalamata or Gaeta
> 2 tablespoons chopped flat-leaf parsley, for garnish

1.   Place the carrots and salt in a large pot and add cold water to cover. Bring to a boil over high heat. Reduce the heat to medium and simmer 3 to 4 minutes, until crisp-tender. Drain immediately but do not rinse with cold water. Transfer to a large, nonreactive serving dish.

2.   In a small bowl, whisk together the oil and lemon juice. Add the cumin, paprika, cinnamon, and cayenne and whisk again. Pour over the carrots and toss gently to coat. Add the olives and toss again. Set aside and marinate at room temperature 1 hour. Serve garnished with parsley. (The dish can be covered and refrigerated for up to 2 days; bring to room temperature and garnish with parsley just before serving.)

Makes 6 servings

Vegetable Pancakes

This is a nice potato pancake variation made easy—all the vegetables can be shredded in the food processor. They're fabulous on their own or served with sour cream and applesauce alongside Beef Brisket (page 120).

Prep time: 45 minutes Cook time: 3 minutes per batch

> 1 pound zucchini, peeled and shredded
>
> 1 pound Russet potatoes, peeled and shredded
>
> 1 pound carrots, peeled and shredded
>
> 1 onion, finely minced
>
> 1/2 cup finely chopped fresh flat-leaf parsley
>
> 1/2 cup unbleached all-purpose flour
>
> 2 large eggs
>
> 1 tablespoon fresh lemon juice
>
> Kosher salt and freshly ground black pepper
>
> Corn or canola oil, for frying
>
> Sour cream, for serving (optional)
>
> Applesauce, for serving (optional)

1. Combine the zucchini, potatoes, carrots, onion, parsley, and flour in a large bowl. Whisk the eggs and lemon juice together and stir into the vegetable mixture. Generously season with salt and pepper and mix well.

2. In a large heavy skillet, heat about 1/4 inch oil over medium-high heat until hot but not smoking. In batches of 3 or 4 pancakes at a time, spoon about 3 tablespoons of the vegetable mixture into the oil and gently flatten with a spatula. Cook, turning only once, 4 to 5 minutes per side, until golden brown. With a slotted spatula, transfer the pancakes to paper towels to drain. Keep warm until serving. Serve the warm pancakes with sour cream and applesauce, if desired.

Makes about 16 three-inch pancakes

Caramelized Root Vegetables

A savory mix of slow-cooked root vegetables is an ideal dish for a simple autumn meal. Gentle oven-roasting allows them to caramelize and develop a full, rounded flavor. It's easy: simply toss potatoes, carrots, parsnips, and shallots with fruity olive oil and roast. Great for advance dinner party planning—great-tasting, too.

Prep time: 10 minutes Roast time: 1 hour 30 minutes

> 8 to 10 unpeeled small red new potatoes (about 2 pounds),
>   halved or quartered
> 12 shallots, peeled
> 6 carrots, peeled and cut into 1-inch pieces
> 4 parsnips (about 1 pound), peeled and cut into 1-inch rounds
> 3 tablespoons extra-virgin olive oil, plus more for serving (optional)
> 1 teaspoon chopped fresh rosemary leaves
> Kosher salt and freshly ground black pepper

1. Preheat the oven to 300° F.

2. In a roasting pan, toss the potatoes, shallots, carrots, and parsnips with the olive oil, rosemary, and salt and pepper to taste. Roast, tossing 2 or 3 times, $1^1/_2$ to 2 hours, until the vegetables are fork-tender.

3. Arrange the vegetables in a shallow bowl or a large platter. Drizzle with a bit of additional olive oil, if desired. Serve warm.

Makes 6 servings

Serving Style

There are many lively, inventive ways to decorate the table other than the standard centerpiece bouquet. Feel free to set your own distinctive personal tone with favorite objects and items from nature.

SMALL ARRANGEMENTS

Individual stems of fresh flowers such as tulips (left) or ranunculus (below) set in small containers look beautiful on the table. They also work very well for a dinner party because they are low— guests won't have to peer around a large arrangement to chat.

NATURAL BEAUTIES

Look no further than the farmers' market for gorgeous table and dining room decor. Simple tall stems (left), kumquats (below left) or Forelli pears (below right) placed in bowls, baskets, or vases add beautiful, vibrant color to the table. More fresh ideas: Granny Smith apples, bright lemons and limes, and fresh cranberries.

Mashed Yukon Golds

Creamy Yukon gold potatoes make smooth, full-bodied mashed potatoes—of course, the butter and sour cream help a little, too.

Prep Time: 15 minutes Cook Time: 20 minutes

> 6 Yukon gold potatoes (about 6 ounces each), peeled and cubed
> ½ cup milk, heated
> 1 tablespoon unsalted butter, at room temperature
> 1 tablespoon sour cream
> Kosher salt and freshly ground black pepper
> 2 tablespoons chopped fresh chives

1. Bring a large saucepan of lightly salted water to a boil over high heat. Add the potatoes and return to a boil. Reduce the heat and simmer about 20 minutes, until the potatoes are fork-tender. Drain and return the potatoes to the saucepan.

2. Using a hand-held electric mixer or a potato masher, mash the potatoes, gradually adding the milk, butter, and sour cream. Season with salt and pepper and mash until smooth. Stir in the chives. Taste and correct the seasonings and serve immediately.

Makes 6 servings

Sweet Potato, Carrot, and Turnip Purée

Make this purée a Thanksgiving tradition at your house. Its rich, full flavor speaks of the holidays.

Prep time: 15 minutes Cook time: 20 minutes

> 1 pound carrots, peeled and coarsely chopped
> 1 pound white turnips, peeled and coarsely chopped
> 1 pound sweet potatoes, peeled and cut into 2-inch pieces
> 2 tablespoons unsalted butter, at room temperature,
>   cut into pieces
> 1/2 cup heavy cream, plus more if necessary
> Kosher salt and freshly ground black pepper

1. Bring a large pot of salted water to a boil. Add the carrots, turnips, and sweet potatoes and cook over medium-high heat until tender, about 20 minutes. Drain well.

2. Combine the vegetables, butter, and 1/4 cup cream in a food processor. Pulse, adding the remaining 1/4 cup cream, until the mixture is very smooth. Add a bit more cream, if the purée seems too thick. Season to taste with salt and pepper.

3. Transfer the purée to a serving dish and serve. (Or transfer to an ovenproof baking dish, cover with foil, and keep warm in a 200° F oven for up 30 minutes.)

Makes 8 servings

Sweet Potato and Red Onion Gratin

Sweet potatoes are especially good baked with red onions in a gratin, and the preparation is minimal—just slice and roast them with apple cider, brown sugar, and fresh thyme.

Prep time: 15 minutes Bake time: 1 hour and 30 minutes

6 medium sweet potatoes (about 3 pounds), peeled and thinly sliced

3 medium red onions, cut into thin round slices

1½ cups apple cider

2 teaspoons light brown sugar

Kosher salt and freshly ground black pepper

1 tablespoon fresh thyme leaves

1 tablespoon unsalted butter, cut into small pieces

1. Preheat the oven to 350° F.
2. In a 11 x 7 gratin dish, arrange the sweet potato and red onion slices in alternate layers.
3. In a small saucepan over medium heat, combine the cider, brown sugar, and salt and pepper to taste. Cook, stirring often, until the sugar dissolves. Pour the cider mixture over the sweet potatoes and onions. Sprinkle with the thyme and dot with the butter.
4. Cover the gratin dish with foil and bake 1 hour. Remove the foil and continue baking, basting often, until the sweet potatoes and onions are tender, about 20 minutes longer. Serve immediately.

Makes 6 servings

Oven-Braised Leeks and Garlic

Leeks and garlic braised in olive oil and broth make a delicious and versatile side dish to serve with all types of meat and fish dishes.

Prep time: 10 minutes Bake time: 60 minutes

> 2 tablespoons olive oil
> 3 large leeks (white and tender green parts), halved, washed well,
>   and cut into thirds
> 6 cloves garlic, halved
> 3 tablespoons chicken broth, plus more if necessary
> Kosher salt and freshly ground black pepper

1. Preheat the oven to 350° F.
2. Coat the bottom of a large baking dish with the olive oil. Arrange the leeks and garlic in the dish. Drizzle with the broth and season with salt and pepper.
3. Bake about 45 minutes, until the leeks are tender but still offering some resistance. Add a little more broth if the leeks seem dry. Bake about 15 minutes longer, until tender. Serve warm or at room temperature.

Makes 6 servings

Vidalia Onions
Baked in Tomato Juice and Molasses

Vidalia onions taste fabulous cooked in so many ways; a favorite is to bake them in tomato juice and molasses. This is a good side with roast pork, ham, or chicken. For a slightly different flavor, use maple syrup instead of molasses.

Prep time: 15 minutes Bake time: 1 hour 30 minutes

> 4 medium Vidalia onions (about 3 pounds)
> 1 cup tomato juice
> 1 cup water
> 2 tablespoons unsalted butter
> 2 tablespoons regular molasses (not blackstrap)
> Kosher salt and freshly ground black pepper

1. Preheat the oven to 400° F.
2. Halve the onions lengthwise, keeping the root ends intact, and peel. Arrange them, cut sides up, in a 9 x 13-inch baking dish.
3. In a saucepan over medium-high heat, bring the tomato juice, water, butter, molasses, and salt and pepper to taste to a boil, stirring occasionally. Pour over the onions.
4. Bake the onions, uncovered, basting every 30 minutes, until browned and very tender, about 1 hour and 30 minutes.

Makes 6 servings

Savory Baked Beans

Slow-cooked baked beans made from scratch are fantastic to serve with Southern-Style Barbecue Chicken (page 140) and Mixed Cabbage Slaw with Horseradish Mayonnaise (page 99) at a summer barbecue or picnic.

Prep time: 15 minutes plus soaking Bake time: 2 hours

1 pound dried baby lima beans

3 slices bacon, coarsely chopped

2 tablespoons olive oil

1 large onion, coarsely chopped

4 cloves garlic, finely chopped

1 (28-ounce) can diced plum tomatoes in purée

1/2 cup packed light brown sugar

1/4 cup Dijon mustard

1 tablespoon finely chopped fresh thyme

Dash hot sauce

Kosher salt and freshly ground black pepper

1 cup chicken broth, plus more if necessary

1. Pick over the beans to remove any small stones or debris; rinse thoroughly. Place the beans in a large bowl, add enough cold water to cover by 2 inches, and soak 6 to 8 hours or overnight. Drain.

2. Preheat the oven to 350° F.

3. In a large soup pot or Dutch oven over medium-high heat, cook the bacon until lightly browned. Add the olive oil, onion, and garlic, and cook, stirring occasionally, until the onion is translucent.

4. Add the tomatoes, brown sugar, mustard, thyme, hot sauce, and salt and pepper to taste; bring to a boil. Reduce the heat, stir well, and simmer 5 minutes. Add the beans and broth and stir well again.

5. Cover and bake 1 hour and 30 minutes. Uncover and bake, stirring in more broth if the beans seem dry, 30 minutes longer, until the beans are just tender. (The beans can be prepared 1 day ahead and refrigerated; reheat before serving.)

Makes 8 servings

Warm Lentils and Spinach

Lentils and spinach taste great together and are an excellent side dish to serve with grilled fish or chicken.

Prep time: 10 minutes Cook time: 30 minutes

> 3 tablespoons olive oil
> 1½ cups dried lentils
> 2¼ cups chicken broth
> ½ cup water
> 2 cloves garlic, thinly sliced
> 10 ounces fresh spinach, washed well, stemmed,
>   and coarsely chopped
> Kosher salt and freshly ground pepper

1. Heat 2 tablespoons olive oil in a large skillet over medium-high heat. Add the lentils and toss to coat with the oil. Add 2 cups broth and the water and bring to a boil. Reduce the heat, cover, and simmer, stirring occasionally, 25 to 30 minutes, until the lentils are just tender.

2. Meanwhile, heat the remaining 1 tablespoon olive oil in another skillet over medium heat. Add the garlic and cook, stirring, 1 to 2 minutes, until softened. Add the spinach and cook, stirring and tossing occasionally, about 1 minute, until it begins to wilt. Add the remaining ¼ cup broth and cook until the spinach is tender and wilted.

3. Add the spinach and any cooking liquid to the lentils and toss together. Season with salt and pepper and serve immediately.

Makes 6 servings

Grilling Vegetables

Vegetables cooked on the grill are a warm-weather favorite and are excellent accompaniments to other grilled foods such as fish, chicken, and steak. When grilling vegetables, be sure to brush them generously with olive oil or marinate them before cooking to eliminate the raw taste that quick grilling might leave.

Grilled Sweet Potatoes with Asian Vinaigrette

Sweet potatoes straight from the grill, drizzled with gingery vinaigrette—heaven! They're great with grilled chicken or fish.

Prep time: 20 minutes Grill/Cook time: 25 minutes

> 4 medium sweet potatoes (about 2 pounds)
> 1/4 cup corn oil, plus more for brushing the grill rack
> 2 tablespoons light soy sauce
>
> Asian Vinaigrette:
> 3/4 cup extra-virgin olive oil
> 1/4 cup rice wine vinegar
> 1 tablespoon light soy sauce
> 2 tablespoons chopped fresh flat-leaf parsley
> 1 tablespoon finely chopped fresh ginger
> 4 scallions, finely minced
>
> Chopped fresh flat-leaf parsley, for garnish

1. Prepare a medium-hot gas or charcoal grill (coals are covered with a light coating of ash and glow deep red). Brush the grill rack with corn oil.
2. Bring a large pot of salted water to a boil over high heat. Add the sweet potatoes and return to a boil. Reduce the heat and simmer until just tender, about 15 minutes. Drain and rinse When the potatoes are cool enough to handle, peel and cut into 1/4-inch slices. Arrange the slices in a single layer in a shallow pan or tray. In a small bowl, whisk together the corn oil and soy sauce. Brush over the potatoes.

3. To make the vinaigrette: In a small bowl, whisk together the olive oil, vinegar, and soy sauce. Stir in the parsley, ginger, and scallions. Set aside.

4. Grill the potatoes, turning often, about 10 minutes. Transfer the potatoes to a shallow bowl or serving platter. Drizzle with the vinaigrette, garnish with the parsley, and serve immediately.

Makes 6 servings

Grilled Vegetable Caponata

Nicely charred and smoky eggplant and onions—mixed with tomatoes, capers, and olives—are fabulous, especially with grilled lamb chops or steak.

Prep time: 20 minutes plus chilling Grill/Cook time: 18 minutes

3 medium eggplants, peeled
 and cut into 1/2-inch-thick slices
2 large red onions, cut into 1/2-inch-thick slices
1/2 cup olive oil
1/2 cup golden raisins
3/4 cup red wine
1 (28-ounce) can plum tomatoes, coarsely chopped,
 with their juice
1/2 cup kalamata olives, pitted and chopped
1/4 cup balsamic vinegar
3 tablespoons drained capers
1/2 cup chopped fresh flat-leaf parsley
Kosher salt and freshly ground black pepper

1. Prepare a medium-hot gas or charcoal grill (coals are covered with a light coating of ash and glow deep red).

2. Preheat the oven to 400° F. Generously brush the eggplant and onion slices with the olive oil and arrange on separate baking sheets. Roast in the oven, turning once, 10 to 15 minutes, until soft.

3. Transfer the eggplant and onions to the grill and cook, turning often, until nicely browned, about 5 minutes. Set aside to cool.

4. Place the raisins in a small saucepan and cover with the wine. Bring to a simmer over medium heat; cook 3 minutes. Set aside to allow the raisins to plump.

5. In a large bowl, combine the raisins and wine, the tomatoes, olives, vinegar, and capers. Chop the grilled eggplant and onions into small pieces and add to the tomato mixture; toss well to combine. Stir in the parsley and salt and pepper to taste. Cover and refrigerate until the mixture mellows, 6 to 8 hours or overnight (or up to 1 week).

6. Before serving, taste and adjust the seasonings. Serve warm, chilled, or at room temperature.

Makes about 6 cups or 12 servings

Grilled Vegetables
with Ricotta-Pesto Sauce

A creamy pesto sauce is a stunning accompaniment to grilled vegetables, which are among the most delicious of all grilled foods. Make the sauce when basil is full and lush in the garden.

Prep time: 20 minutes Grill time: 8 minutes

Ricotta-Pesto Sauce:
3/4 cup firmly packed fresh basil leaves
1/2 cup extra-virgin olive oil
1/4 cup pine nuts
1 clove garlic, coarsely chopped
Pinch kosher salt
1/3 cup ricotta cheese
1/2 cup mascarpone cheese

3 zucchini, cut lengthwise into 1-inch-thick pieces
3 fennel bulbs, trimmed and cut lengthwise
    into 1/4-inch-thick slices
2 red bell peppers, halved, seeded, deveined,
    and cut into 1/4-inch-wide strips
2 yellow bell peppers, halved, seeded, deveined,
    and cut into 1/4-inch-wide strips
1/4 cup extra-virgin olive oil
Kosher salt and freshly ground black pepper

1. To make the sauce: Place the basil, olive oil, pine nuts, garlic, and salt in the bowl of a food processor fitted with a steel blade. Process until smooth, scraping down the sides of the bowl as needed. Add the ricotta and mascarpone cheeses and pulse just until combined. (The sauce can be covered and refrigerated for up to 3 hours; bring to room temperature before serving.)

2. Prepare a medium-hot gas or charcoal grill (coals are covered with a light coating of ash and glow deep red). Lightly spray the grill rack with vegetable oil spray.

3. Brush the zucchini, fennel, and red and yellow bell peppers generously with the olive oil and season with salt and pepper. Lay the zucchini and fennel on the grill rack and grill, turning once, about 8 minutes, until lightly charred and tender. Grill the peppers, turning once, about 4 minutes, until lightly charred and tender.

4. Spoon the sauce into a bowl and set it in the center of a large platter. Surround it with the grilled vegetables and serve.

Makes 6 to 8 servings

Wild Rice with Toasted Walnuts

Nutty and aromatic wild rice goes well with all types of meat, poultry, and fish. The general rule of thumb when cooking wild rice is three parts liquid to one part rice—however, different brands and styles of wild rice can vary, so it is best to read and follow package directions carefully.

Prep time: 20 minutes Cook time: 45 minutes

> 1 cup wild rice, rinsed and drained
> 2 cups water
> 1 cup chicken broth
> 1 tablespoon unsalted butter or olive oil
> 1/3 cup chopped walnuts, lightly toasted (see page 109)
> Kosher salt and freshly ground black pepper

1. Combine the wild rice, water, broth, and butter in a pan with a tight-fitting lid and bring to a boil. Reduce the heat, cover, and simmer 45 minutes. Do not remove the lid. Remove from the heat and let sit 10 minutes. Or cook the wild rice according to package directions.
2. Before serving, fluff the rice with a fork, stir in the walnuts, and toss well. Season with salt and pepper and serve immediately.

Makes 6 servings

Barley Risotto

Barley risotto has a richer, nuttier flavor than traditional risotto made with Arborio rice—and it's less time-consuming! It is made in the same manner: Pearl barley is sautéed in oil with vegetables and then simmered while hot broth is added, ladleful by ladleful. It pairs very nicely with roasted lamb or fish.

Prep time: 10 minutes Cook time: 30 minutes

4 cups chicken broth
2 tablespoons olive oil
1 onion, finely diced
1 rib celery, finely diced
1 carrot, peeled and finely diced
1 cup pearl barley
1/2 cup dry white wine
Kosher salt and freshly ground black pepper
1/2 cup chopped fresh flat-leaf parsley, for garnish

1. In a saucepan, bring the broth to a boil over high heat. Reduce the heat to low and simmer while making the risotto.

2. Heat the olive oil in a large sauté pan over medium-high heat. Add the onion, celery, and carrot and cook about 5 minutes, until just softened. Add the barley and cook, stirring constantly, 1 minute. Add the wine and cook, stirring constantly, 3 to 4 minutes, until the wine is reduced slightly.

3. Add 2 ladlefuls of hot broth (about 1/2 cup) to the barley, stirring constantly, until the barley absorbs nearly all the liquid. Continue stirring and adding broth, a ladleful or two at a time and not adding the next ladle until the previous one is absorbed by the barley. When nearly all the broth has been added, the barley will be slightly creamy and just tender. This will take about 20 minutes.

4. Season with salt and pepper and mix gently. Garnish with the parsley and serve immediately.

Makes 6 servings

Buttermilk-Chive Biscuits

Mixing onion-y chives into biscuit dough yields savory, aromatic biscuits that taste great with grilled meat and poultry. For plain biscuits, just omit the chives.

Prep time: 35 minutes Bake time: 10 minutes

> 2 cups unbleached all-purpose flour
> 1 tablespoon baking powder
> 1 teaspoon salt
> 6 tablespoons unsalted butter, cut into pieces and chilled
> 2/3 cup buttermilk
> 2 tablespoons chopped fresh chives

1. Preheat the oven to 450° F.
2. In a large bowl, whisk together the flour, baking powder, and salt. Cut the butter into the flour mixture using your fingertips, a pastry blender, or two knives, working it until the mixture resembles coarse crumbs. Add the buttermilk all at once and stir to mix until the dough holds together. Stir in the chives.
3. Turn the dough out onto a lightly floured surface and knead 2 or 3 times until it holds together; do not overwork. With lightly floured hands, pat the dough into a circle about 1/4-inch thick. Using a 2- or 2 1/2-inch biscuit cutter or drinking glass, cut out as many biscuits as you can. Arrange the biscuits 1 inch apart on an ungreased baking sheet. Gather the dough scraps together and pat the dough out again, cutting more biscuits.
4. Bake the biscuits 10 to 15 minutes, until risen and lightly browned. Serve hot.

Makes 10 to 12 biscuits

Variations

For taller biscuits, pat the dough into a circle about 1/2 inch thick; bake 12 to 17 minutes. You will only get 8 to 10 biscuits, but they will be fluffier and higher. For even taller biscuits, pat the dough into a fatter circle, between 1/2- and 1 inch thick; bake 15 to 20 minutes. You will get 6 to 8 biscuits that are very tall but run the risk of not cooking all the way through.

Red Pepper Cornbread

Cornbread studded with sweet red pepper is great to serve with hot soup or stew, or as an accompaniment to barbecued chicken or ribs. If you prefer plain cornbread, omit the red peppers. Either way, it's a winner.

Prep time: 50 minutes Bake time: 30 minutes

> 2 medium red bell peppers
> 2 tablespoons unsalted butter
> 1 cup stone-ground yellow cornmeal
> 1 cup unbleached all-purpose flour
> 2 tablespoons sugar
> 2 teaspoons baking powder
> 1/2 teaspoon kosher salt
> 2 large eggs
> 1 cup milk

1. Preheat the broiler. Place the peppers on a baking sheet a few inches from the heat and roast until charred, turning several times. Transfer to a small paper bag and fold to seal. Set aside to let the peppers cool inside the bag for at least 20 minutes. When cool, rub the charred skin from the peppers and cut each in half. Scrape out the seeds, cut off the stems, and cut the flesh into 1/2-inch pieces; set aside. You will have about 1 cup.

2. Preheat the oven to 400° F. Place the butter in an 8-inch-round baking dish and place the dish in the oven while preparing the batter; be careful that the butter does not burn.

3. In a large bowl, whisk together the cornmeal, flour, sugar, baking powder, and salt. In a small bowl, mix the eggs with the milk. Pour the egg-milk mixture into the cornmeal mixture and stir with a fork until well blended. Stir in the red peppers.

4. Remove the baking dish from the oven and scrape the batter into it. Stir gently to incorporate the melted butter; smooth the top. Bake about 20 minutes, until the bread pulls away from the sides of the pan, the top is set, and a toothpick inserted in the center comes out clean. Let cool on a wire rack. Cut into squares and serve.

Makes 6 to 8 servings

Cranberry Relish with Blood Orange Juice and Dried Cherries

Cranberry relish is not just for Thanksgiving! This tasty, tart version is a nice surprise and adds a lovely touch to any meal. Look for blood oranges, which have bright red flesh and wonderful sweet-tart juice. They are available in fall and winter, and are sometimes called Maltese oranges. You can also use navel orange juice in this recipe.

Prep time: 10 minutes plus chilling Cook time: 10 minutes

> 12 ounces fresh cranberries, rinsed
> 2/3 cup sugar
> 2/3 cup fresh blood orange juice or other sweet orange juice
> 1/3 cup water
> 1/2 cup plus 2 tablespoons dried cherries
> 2 tablespoons Grand Marnier

1. In a heavy saucepan, combine the cranberries, sugar, orange juice, and water and bring to a boil over high heat. Reduce the heat and simmer gently about 10 minutes, until the cranberries begin to pop.

2. Remove from the heat and stir in the dried cherries and Grand Marnier. Cool, cover, and refrigerate for at least 1 hour (or up to 1 week). Serve chilled.

Makes about 4 cups

Tomato-Ginger Relish

This is a fabulous condiment to spread over all types of grilled meat and fish.

Prep time: 10 minutes Cook time: 40 minutes

> 1½ cups water
> 1½ cups peeled, chopped ginger
> 1 large ripe tomato, coarsely chopped
> ½ cup sugar, or to taste
> 5 cloves garlic, chopped
> 1 dried chile or pinch red pepper flakes
> Kosher salt and freshly ground black pepper

Combine the water, ginger, tomato, sugar, garlic, chile, and salt and pepper to taste in a saucepan. Bring to a boil, reduce the heat and simmer, stirring occasionally, until very thick, 40 to 45 minutes. Remove the chile (if using), taste, and adjust the seasonings. (The relish can be covered and refrigerated for up to 3 days; bring to room temperature before serving.)

Makes about 1½ cups

Serving Style

Side dishes should always look (and taste!) as special as the main course. A great meal is not complete without a few well-cooked and thoughtfully served sides.

SERVING SPOONS

Casual serving spoons (right) look great and set just the right tone for an outdoor buffet. You can never go wrong with silver serving utensils and oversize hotel linen napkins (below).

YEAR-ROUND VEGETABLES

Vegetables such as beets, carrots, broccoli, and onions are always good choices for entertaining because they are fresh and available the entire year. Depending on the season, these versatile and delicious vegetables can be steamed, sautéed, or slow-roasted and served warm, cold, or at room temperature.

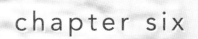

chapter six
Desserts

desserts

Whether you are serving a show-stopping layer cake, a holiday pie, a comfort-food pudding, or a simple bowl of berries or fruit, dessert is always a welcome indulgence for everyone at the table. Celebrate and enjoy!

Chocolate Layer Cake with Raspberry Sauce

For chocolate dessert lovers, this cake is the real deal. It's made with rich and indulgent layers of chocolate cake, coated with swirls of chocolate frosting and topped with raspberry sauce. Your dinner guests will be dazzled.

Prep time: 45 minutes plus chilling Bake time: 30 minutes

Cake:

1 3/4 cups unbleached all-purpose flour

1 1/2 teaspoons baking soda

1/2 teaspoon baking powder

Pinch kosher salt

4 ounces unsweetened chocolate, coarsely chopped

1 cup (2 sticks) unsalted butter

1 cup hot water

2 cups granulated sugar

2 large eggs, at room temperature

1 teaspoon pure vanilla extract

Raspberry Sauce:

2 (10-ounce) packages frozen raspberries in light syrup, partially thawed

1 tablespoon plus 1 teaspoon arrowroot

1 tablespoon orange juice, Grand Marnier, or Cointreau

Frosting:

12 ounces bittersweet chocolate, coarsely chopped

9 ounces cream cheese, softened

1 cup (2 sticks) unsalted butter, softened

1 cup confectioners' sugar

1 teaspoon pure vanilla extract

1. Preheat the oven to 350° F. Lightly butter and flour two 9-inch cake pans; tap out the excess flour.

2. To make the cake: In a bowl, combine the flour, baking soda, baking powder, and salt and whisk 8 to 10 times until well mixed. In the top of a double boiler set over barely simmering water, combine the unsweetened chocolate, butter, and water, and stir until the mixture is smooth and the chocolate is melted. Transfer to a mixing bowl and stir in the granulated sugar. Cool to lukewarm.

3. Using an electric mixer set on medium speed, beat the eggs into the chocolate mixture, one at a time, until well mixed. Add the vanilla and beat just to mix. Gradually add the flour mixture, mixing on low speed or stirring by hand, until the batter is smooth.

4. Divide the batter evenly between the prepared pans and tap gently on the countertop to burst any air bubbles and distribute evenly. Bake on the center racks of the oven about 30 minutes, until the centers spring back when lightly touched and the edges of the cakes pull away from the sides of the pans. Cool the cakes in the pans set on wire racks about 5 minutes and then turn out onto the racks to cool completely.

5. To make the sauce: Drain the raspberries in a sieve set over a bowl, reserving the juice. Transfer the raspberries to a glass or ceramic bowl and set aside. Set aside 1 cup of the juice and discard the rest. In a small cup, combine the arrowroot with 1 tablespoon reserved juice and stir until smooth. Stir this mixture into the remaining juice and transfer to a nonreactive saucepan. Bring to a boil over medium-high heat, stirring constantly, cooking 30 to 60 seconds only. Remove from the heat and stir in the orange juice. Pour the heated mixture over the raspberries and stir gently until mixed. Cover and refrigerate until chilled, at least 1 hour (or up to 2 days).

6. To make the frosting: In the top of a double boiler set over barely simmering water, melt the bittersweet chocolate, stirring until smooth. Remove the top of the double boiler from the heat and let the chocolate cool to lukewarm, about 5 minutes. In a large bowl with an electric mixer set on medium-high speed, beat the cream cheese and butter until smooth. Add the confectioners' sugar, about 1/4 cup at a time, and beat 1 to 2 minutes, until smooth. Add the vanilla and melted chocolate and continue beating about 1 minute, until well mixed and fluffy. Cover and set aside at room temperature until ready to use.

7. To assemble the cake: Trim the cake layers so that one will sit evenly on top of the other. Spread about 1/2 cup frosting over the bottom layer and set the second layer on top. Frost the sides and top of the cake generously. Cut into wedges and serve, passing the chilled raspberry sauce at the table.

Makes 8 to 12 servings

Lining the Pans with Waxed Paper

If you take the extra step of lining the buttered and floured baking pans with waxed paper and then butter and flour the paper, the cake layers will be easier to remove from the pan. Once the cakes are removed from the pans, peel the waxed paper from the layers and let the cakes cool.

Apple-Walnut Cake with Caramel Sauce

Usher in autumn with a fantastic cake made with the season's best apples.

Prep time: 20 minutes Bake time: 50 minutes

Apple-Walnut Cake:

4 large eggs

1½ cups packed light brown sugar

¼ cup corn oil

1½ teaspoons pure vanilla extract

2 cups unbleached all-purpose flour

1½ teaspoons baking soda

1 teaspoon grated nutmeg

1 teaspoon ground cinnamon

1 teaspoon grated lemon zest

½ teaspoon kosher salt

1 pound baking apples, peeled, cored, and finely chopped

1¼ cups toasted walnuts (see page 109), finely chopped

Warm Caramel Sauce:

1 cup heavy cream

1 cup sugar

1 cup water

1 large egg

1 large egg yolk

2 tablespoons strong coffee or espresso

1 teaspoon pure vanilla extract

2 tablespoons unsalted butter, at room temperature

Whipped cream, for serving

1. To make the cake: Preheat the oven to 350° F. Lightly butter and flour a 10-inch springform pan; tap out the excess flour.

2. In a large bowl, whisk together the eggs, brown sugar, oil, and vanilla. Add the flour, baking soda, nutmeg, cinnamon, lemon zest, salt, apples, and walnuts and stir until just combined. Pour the batter into the prepared pan. Bake on the middle rack of the oven about 50 minutes, until a cake tester inserted in the middle comes out clean.

3.   Meanwhile, make the caramel sauce: Heat the cream in a small saucepan over medium-low heat. In a heavy-bottomed saucepan, combine the sugar and water and mix well. Cook over medium heat, stirring once with a wooden spoon, until the sugar is a rich golden brown. Remove from the heat. Add the warm cream to the caramelized sugar and return to the heat. Cook 3 minutes, being careful not to let the mixture boil over. Let cool 15 minutes. Stir in the egg, egg yolk, coffee, and vanilla. Stir in the butter. Let the sauce cool completely. (The sauce can be covered and refrigerated for up to 1 day; bring to room temperature before reheating.)

4.   Remove the cake from the pan and cut into wedges. Gently reheat the caramel sauce over low heat. Spoon the sauce onto 8 or 10 dessert plates and top with wedges of cake. Garnish with whipped cream and serve.

Makes 8 to 10 servings

Peaches and Cream Birthday Cake

Here is a wonderful birthday cake to make for a late summer party. It's frosted with nothing more than freshly whipped cream and served with the season's juiciest and sweetest peaches.

Prep time: 40 minutes Bake time: 30 minutes

3 cups unbleached all-purpose flour

1 tablespoon baking powder

1/2 teaspoon kosher salt

3/4 cup (1 1/2 sticks) unsalted butter, at room temperature

2 cups sugar

1 teaspoon pure vanilla extract

1 cup milk

6 large egg whites, at room temperature

1 cup heavy cream

1 tablespoon sugar

6 to 8 ripe peaches, peeled and sliced into thin wedges

1. Preheat the oven to 375° F. Lightly butter and flour two 9-inch cake pans; tap out the excess flour.

2. In a large bowl, whisk together the flour, baking powder, and salt. In another large bowl, using an electric mixer set on high speed, cream the butter and 1 1/2 cups sugar about 2 minutes, until light and fluffy. Add the vanilla and beat until just combined. With the mixer running on medium speed, add about 3/4 cup flour mixture and then 1/4 cup milk. Repeat three times until all the flour and milk is used. Beat until the batter is smooth; do not overmix.

3. In a large, clean dry bowl with clean beaters, beat the egg whites on medium-high speed until foamy. Increase the speed to high and slowly add the remaining 1/2 cup sugar. Beat until stiff peaks form. Gently fold into the cake batter.

4. Divide the batter between the prepared pans. Smooth the tops with a spatula. Bake the cake layers 30 to 35 minutes, until a cake tester inserted in the middle of each comes out clean and the cakes are golden brown and begin to pull away from the sides of the pans. Let the cake layers cool in their pans about 5 minutes. Loosen the edges with a knife and invert the layers onto wire racks to cool completely.

5. Shortly before serving, in a large bowl with an electric mixer set on high speed, whip the cream and sugar until lightly whipped; it should hold its shape when mounded.

6. Spread some whipped cream on top of one cooled cake layer. Place the second layer on top. Spread the remaining whipped cream over the top and sides of the cake. (The cake can be refrigerated for up to 2 hours before serving.) To serve, garnish the top of the cake with peach slices, cut into 12 wedges, and serve.

Makes 12 servings

Ricotta-Almond Cheesecake

The light taste and texture of cheesecake made with ricotta cheese instead of the more common cream cheese is amazing. This is a fabulous dessert on its own, but it's great to serve with fresh berries or peaches as well.

Prep time: 25 minutes plus draining Bake time: 1 hour 10 minutes

    4 cups ricotta cheese
    1 1/2 cups graham cracker crumbs (from about 20 squares)
    6 tablespoons (3/4 stick) unsalted butter, melted
    3/4 cup sugar
    4 large eggs
    1 cup heavy cream
    1/3 cup finely chopped almonds
    1 teaspoon almond extract

1. Place the ricotta in a sieve over a bowl and let drain 1 hour.
2. Preheat the oven to 350° F. Lightly butter a 9-inch springform pan. In a mixing bowl, combine the crumbs, melted butter, and 1/4 cup sugar. Blend well. Transfer to the prepared springform pan and press with the back of a wooden spoon or your fingertips to evenly cover the bottom and partway up the sides of the pan. Bake the crust 10 minutes. Cool completely on a wire rack.
3. Reduce the heat to 325° F.
4. In a large mixing bowl with an electric mixer on low speed, beat the drained ricotta and remaining 1/2 cup sugar. Beat in the eggs, one at a time, until smooth. Add the cream, almonds, and almond extract and beat until smooth. Pour into the prepared crust. Bake the cheesecake until the center is firm, 1 hour. Cool to room temperature in the pan on a rack, then refrigerate until chilled, at least 2 hours (or up to 24 hours).
5. Remove the cheesecake from the pan by releasing the sides; transfer to a plate.

Makes 6 to 8 servings

Lemon-Buttermilk Pie
with Fresh Strawberries

This easy-to-prepare pie is best if served on the same day it's made. To prevent the filling from separating, be sure to have all the ingredients at room temperature.

Prep time: 20 minutes plus standing Bake time: 30 minutes

1½ pints fresh strawberries, stemmed and thinly sliced

1 cup plus 1 tablespoon sugar

2 tablespoons port

3 large eggs

Grated zest of 1 lemon

3 tablespoons fresh lemon juice

1 teaspoon pure vanilla extract

½ teaspoon kosher salt

1 cup buttermilk

6 tablespoons (¾ stick) unsalted butter,
  melted and cooled

1 (9-inch) pie crust, baked and cooled

1. In a large bowl, toss the strawberries with 1 tablespoon sugar and the port; let stand at room temperature 1 to 2 hours.

2. Preheat the oven to 400° F.

3. In a large bowl, mix the eggs with a fork until light. Gradually add the remaining 1 cup sugar and mix until very smooth. Mix in the lemon zest, lemon juice, vanilla, and salt. Continue mixing, slowly adding the buttermilk and melted butter. Mix until smooth.

4. Pour the mixture into the pie crust. Bake 10 minutes. Reduce the heat to 350° F and bake 20 to 25 minutes longer, until the center of the filling is still a bit loose (it will continue to cook as it cools). Allow the pie to cool completely before serving.

5. Cut into wedges and serve with strawberries on top of each slice.

Makes 6 to 8 servings

Brandied Pumpkin Pie with Gingersnap Crust

Everyone at the holiday table will love this luscious pie. Serve with vanilla ice cream or whipped cream.

Prep time: 30 minutes Bake time: 50 minutes

Crust:

2 cups finely crushed gingersnap cookies (from about 30 cookies)

1 tablespoon granulated sugar

4 tablespoons (1/2 stick) unsalted butter, melted

Filling:

1 cup canned unsweetened pumpkin

3/4 cup evaporated milk

3 large eggs

1 cup lightly packed light brown sugar

1 teaspoon ground cinnamon

1/2 teaspoon ground ginger

1/2 teaspoon ground nutmeg

1/4 teaspoon ground cloves

1/4 cup brandy or cognac

1.   Preheat the oven to 325° F. Generously butter a 10-inch glass or ceramic tart or pie pan.
2.   To prepare the crust: In a bowl, toss the gingersnap crumbs with the granulated sugar. Add the butter and stir with a wooden spoon or work with your fingertips until the crumbs are moistened. Transfer to the prepared tart pan and press with the back of a wooden spoon or your fingertips to evenly cover the bottom and sides of the pan. Bake for about 8 minutes, until very lightly browned. Cool completely on a wire rack.
3.   To make the filling: In a mixing bowl, combine the pumpkin, evaporated milk, and eggs and mix well with a spoon. Mix in the brown sugar, cinnamon, ginger, nutmeg, and cloves. Add the brandy and mix thoroughly.
4.   Spoon the filling into the crust and spread evenly. Bake the pie 40 to 45 minutes, until a knife inserted in the center comes out clean. Serve warm or cooled.

Makes 6 to 8 servings

Pear Tart

This simple and elegant tart, made with red Bartlett pears, is lovely to serve for dessert.

Prep time: 35 minutes plus chilling Bake time: 1 hour

Pastry Dough:
1¾ cups unbleached all-purpose flour
10 tablespoons (1¼ sticks) unsalted butter, chilled, cut into pieces
1 tablespoon vegetable shortening, chilled, cut into pieces
1 teaspoon kosher salt
5 to 8 tablespoons ice water

Pear Filling:
4 to 5 red Bartlett pears, peeled, cored, and thinly sliced
3 tablespoons fresh lemon juice
3 tablespoons sugar
1 tablespoon cornstarch
½ teaspoon grated nutmeg
¾ cup seedless raspberry jam or currant jelly, melted

1. To prepare the dough: Combine the flour, butter, shortening, and salt in the bowl of a food processor fitted with a steel blade. Pulse 4 to 5 times to break up the fat. With the machine running, add 5 tablespoons ice water. Turn the food processor off; pulse 5 or 6 times. The dough should begin to mass on the blade. If not, add another tablespoon of water, or more as needed, and pulse. When the dough holds together in a cohesive mass, it is done; do not overmix. Turn the dough out onto the countertop and flatten with the palm of your hand. Dust lightly with flour and wrap in plastic wrap or waxed paper. Refrigerate 1 to 2 hours.

2. Preheat the oven to 350° F.

3. On a lightly floured work surface or piece of waxed paper with a floured rolling pin, roll the dough into an approximate 10 x 14-inch rectangle. Line an 8 x 11-inch tart pan with the dough, allowing excess dough to hang over the sides. Trim the excess and crimp the edges. Arrange the pears on the dough in 3 rows, filling the pan in a single layer. Sprinkle with the lemon juice. In a small bowl, combine the sugar, cornstarch, and nutmeg and mix well. Sift evenly over the pears.

4. Bake the tart for 1 hour, until the crust is golden brown and the filling is gently bubbling. Set on a wire rack to cool slightly. Loosen the edges of the tart and slide it onto a serving platter. Spoon the melted jam over the tart and let cool completely before serving.

Makes 6 to 8 servings

Serving Style

Cakes, pies, tarts—indeed, all types of desserts—look even more inviting when they are served with beautiful silver and flowers.

SINGLE FLOWERS

Cuttings of single roses (right) and peonies (below) look stunning in small silver bowls and julep cups.

AFTER-DINNER COFFEE, DESSERT WINE, AND LIQUEUR

For a change of pace, serve coffee and after-dinner drinks in the living room, giving your guests a chance to move about and enjoy another setting. Sauternes (left) in small tulip-shaped glasses is an elegant offering. Other dessert wines, as well as brandy, cognac, and eaux de vie, are also lovely to serve.

Peach-Berry Cobbler

Celebrate high summer with luscious peaches, raspberries, blueberries, and blackberries baked with a simple cobbler topping. If some berries are not available, feel free to use any combination to make $1^1/_2$ cups.

Prep time: 40 minutes Bake time: 35 minutes

Filling:

6 ripe peaches (about $2^1/_2$ pounds), peeled, pitted, and thinly sliced

$1^1/_2$ cups fresh raspberries, blueberries, and/or blackberries

$^1/_2$ cup sugar

Topping:

2 cups flour

3 tablespoons sugar, plus extra for sprinkling

$^1/_2$ teaspoon salt

$2^1/_2$ teaspoons baking powder

$^1/_2$ teaspoon grated lemon zest

6 tablepoons unsweetened butter, chilled and cut into small pieces

$^3/_4$ cup heavy cream, plus extra for brushing

1. Preheat the oven to 350° F.
2. To make the filling: Combine the peaches and berries in a large bowl. Sprinkle with the sugar and toss. Set aside at room temperature for about 15 minutes to give juices time to accumulate and sweeten.
3. To make the topping: Put the flour, sugar, salt, baking powder, and lemon zest in a food processor and pulse to mix. Add the butter and pulse 2 or 3 times to cut butter into pea-size pieces.
4. Transfer the mixture to a large bowl, make a well in the center and add the cream, stirring with a wooden spoon or rubber spatula until incorporated.
5. Divide the filling among six 3-inch ramekins. Crumble pieces of the topping to cover the filling and the top of the ramekins. Brush the topping with some additional heavy cream and sprinkle with additional sugar.
6. Bake until the topping is golden brown and the filling is bubbling, about 20 minutes.

Makes 6 to 8 servings

Bread Pudding with Rum-Raisin Sauce

Homey bread pudding is comfort food at its best. You can use any good-quality bread, although baguettes work best.

Prep time: 15 minutes Bake time: 45 minutes

Pudding:
1/2 cup (1 stick) unsalted butter, softened
16 (1/2-inch-thick) slices day-old French bread
3 large eggs
3/4 cup plus 2 tablespoons sugar
4 cups milk
2 tablespoons pure vanilla extract
1/2 teaspoon ground nutmeg, plus more for sprinkling

Rum-Raisin Sauce:
1 1/2 cups water
1/4 cup sugar
1/3 cup raisins
2 tablespoons unsalted butter
1 teaspoon unbleached all-purpose flour
1/4 cup dark rum
2 tablespoons fresh lemon juice

1. To make the pudding: Preheat the oven to 325° F. Butter a large baking dish.
2. Generously butter the bread slices and arrange, buttered side up, in a single layer in the baking dish so that they completely cover the bottom. In a large bowl, whisk the eggs with 3/4 cup sugar until smooth. Slowly add the milk, whisking constantly. Add the vanilla and nutmeg and whisk until mixed. Carefully pour the egg mixture over the bread; sprinkle with the remaining 2 tablespoons sugar. Sprinkle a little more nutmeg over the top, if desired.
3. Place the baking dish in a larger roasting pan. Place the roasting pan in the oven and add enough boiling water to the pan to come halfway up the sides of the dish. Bake 45 to 50 minutes, until the custard is set.

4. To make the sauce: Combine the water and sugar in a saucepan and bring to a boil over medium-high heat. Reduce the heat to medium, add the raisins, and simmer for about 15 minutes to plump. In a separate saucepan, melt the butter over medium heat. Add the flour and cook, stirring constantly, until smooth. Slowly stir in the raisin mixture; bring to a boil. Add the rum and lemon juice and cook, stirring, just until boiling. Remove from the heat. (The sauce can be cooled, covered, and refrigerated for up to 1 day; warm over low heat, stirring well, just before serving.)

5. Cut the pudding into squares and serve with the warm sauce spooned over the top.

Makes 10 to 12 servings

Chocolate-Espresso Mousse with Fresh Strawberries

A simple chocolate mousse, flavored with espresso and topped with fresh strawberries, is an elegant and rich dessert.

Prep time: 25 minutes plus chilling

> 1 (6-ounce) package semisweet chocolate chips
> 4 large eggs, at room temperature, separated
> 2 teaspoons sugar
> 1/2 cup brewed espresso or strong coffee
> 2/3 cup heavy cream
> 12 to 16 fresh strawberries, sliced, for garnish

1. Melt the chocolate in the top of a double boiler set over barely simmering water, stirring until smooth. (Or melt the chocolate in the microwave: Place the chocolate chips in a microwave-safe measuring cup and microwave on medium [50 percent] power about 1 minute. Stir and continue to microwave about 1 minute longer, until the chips soften and look shiny; they will not melt completely. Remove from the microwave and stir until smooth.) Set aside to cool slightly.

2. In a large bowl with an electric mixer set on medium speed, beat the egg yolks and sugar until pale yellow. Stir in the melted chocolate and espresso until well mixed.

3. In another bowl, with the mixer's wire whip or beaters on high speed, whip the cream until stiff peaks form. Using a rubber spatula, gently fold the whipped cream into the chocolate mixture.

4. In a clean dry bowl with the mixer and a clean dry whisk or beaters at high speed, beat the egg whites until stiff peaks form. Using a rubber spatula, gently fold the whites into the chocolate mousse, taking care to incorporate them thoroughly.

5. Spoon the mousse into a large serving bowl or individual dessert bowls or goblets. Chill in the refrigerator overnight. Serve garnished with strawberries.

Makes 6 to 8 servings

Chocolate-Walnut Brownies

Brownies are a favorite with most everyone and always sure to please. They're also very versatile—turn them into an elaborate dessert sundae with ice cream and various toppings, or simply eat them by hand.

Prep time: 25 minutes plus cooling Bake time: 35 minutes

> 5 ounces good-quality unsweetened chocolate
> 1/2 cup (1 stick) unsalted butter, at room temperature
> 1 1/4 cups granulated sugar
> 1/2 teaspoon pure vanilla extract
> 3 large eggs, at room temperature
> 3/4 cups unbleached all-purpose flour
> 1/2 cup walnuts, chopped
> Confectioners' sugar, for garnish

1. Preheat the oven to 325° F. Butter and flour an 8-inch square baking pan. Tap out the excess flour.

2. In the top of a double boiler set over barely simmering water, combine the chocolate and butter and stir until smooth and melted. Remove from the heat and let cool 5 minutes.

3. In a medium bowl with an electric mixer on medium speed, beat the chocolate mixture and granulated sugar until well blended and smooth, about 30 seconds. Scrape down the sides of the bowl with a rubber spatula. Stir in the vanilla. With the mixer on low speed, add the eggs one at a time. After the eggs are well incorporated, scrape the bowl again. Blend until the mixture is very smooth, about 20 seconds. Add the flour and mix well by hand. Stir in the walnuts.

4. Spread the batter evenly in the prepared pan. Bake on the center oven rack about 35 minutes, just until a thin crust forms on the top and a knife inserted in the center comes out clean. Cool in the pan on a wire rack 1 hour.

5. To serve, sift a bit of confectioners' sugar over the top of the brownies and cut into squares.

Makes 16 brownies

Luscious Lemon Wafers

These crisp cookies are delicious with ice cream or sorbet; they're also perfect for dipping into hot coffee after dinner. They keep very well in an airtight container until ready to serve.

Prep time: 15 minutes Bake time: 10 minutes per batch

6 tablespoons (³/₄ stick) unsalted butter, at room temperature

1 cup granulated sugar

1 large egg, at room temperature

1¹/₄ cups unbleached all-purpose flour

4 ounces almonds, ground

1¹/₂ tablespoons fresh lemon juice

1.   Preheat the oven to 350° F. Lightly butter 2 baking sheets.
2.   In a large bowl with an electric mixer on medium speed, beat the butter, sugar, and egg until smooth. Beat in the flour, almonds, and lemon juice and mix until well combined.
3.   Drop the dough by tablespoons, 2 inches apart, onto the baking sheets. Press into 2¹/₂-inch rounds with floured fingers. Bake in batches on the middle rack of the oven 10 to 12 minutes, until the edges are lightly browned. Transfer the cookies with a metal spatula to racks to cool. When cool, store the cookies in an airtight container for up to 5 days.

Makes 2 dozen cookies

Fresh Berries with Mascarpone Cream

Mascarpone is a creamy, buttery-rich cheese from the Lombardy region of Italy. When mixed with a bit of yogurt, sugar, and vanilla, it makes a fantastic topping for fresh berries. If blackberries are in short supply, use fresh blueberries or raspberries.

Prep time: 10 minutes plus chilling

Mascarpone Cream:
1/3 cup mascarpone
1 tablespoon sugar
1/2 teaspoon pure vanilla extract
2/3 cup plain nonfat yogurt

Berries:
4 cups fresh blackberries
1/4 cup crème de cassis
2 tablespoons sugar
1 tablespoon fresh lemon juice

1. To make the mascarpone cream: Whisk together the mascarpone, sugar, and vanilla. Add the yogurt and stir until smooth. Cover and refrigerate for at least 1 hour (or up to 2 days).

2. To prepare the berries: In a large bowl, combine the berries, crème de cassis, sugar, and lemon juice; stir gently but thoroughly. If not serving immediately, cover and refrigerate for up to 1 hour.

3. Spoon the berries into goblets or decorative glass dessert bowls and top with the chilled cream. Serve immediately.

Makes 6 servings

Blood Orange Compote

Blood oranges get their name from the unusual red color of their flesh. Usually available in the spring, they are slightly tart and make a delicious, fresh-tasting dessert.

Prep time: 15 minutes Cook time: 6 minutes

> 4 blood oranges or other sweet oranges
> 1/4 cup orange juice
> 2 tablespoons sugar
> 1/2 teaspoon ground cinnamon
> 1/4 cup coarsely chopped walnuts
> Fresh mint sprigs, for garnish

1. With a fine grater, grate 1 teaspoon zest from one of the oranges; set aside. With a vegetable peeler, remove three 2-inch-long strips of zest from another orange. Cut each strip in half lengthwise. Reserve for garnish.

2. Peel all the oranges and cut away the white pith. Holding the oranges over a bowl to catch the juices, cut the oranges into segments. Transfer the orange segments and the collected juices to a nonreactive saucepan. Add the orange juice, sugar, and cinnamon and bring to a boil over medium-high heat, stirring gently. Stir in the grated zest, reduce the heat, and simmer 6 to 7 minutes, until slightly thickened. Stir in the walnuts and remove from the heat. Set aside to cool. (The compote can be covered and refrigerated up to 2 days.)

3. To serve, spoon the compote into small bowls and garnish with strips of zest and mint sprigs.

Makes 6 servings

Vanilla-Scented Poached Pears

A vanilla bean adds a subtle sweet flavor to ruby-red, wine-poached pears. Note that you need to make this a day ahead to allow the flavors to develop.

Prep time: 10 minutes plus chilling Cook time: 30 minutes

6 Bosc pears, peeled, with stems intact
1/2 cup sugar
4 cups fruity red wine
1/3 cup crème de cassis
2 tablespoons fresh lemon juice
1 vanilla bean, split lengthwise
6 whole cloves

1. Trim the bottom of the pears so they sit upright. Place in a large nonreactive saucepan. In a small bowl, combine the sugar, wine, crème de cassis, and lemon juice. Pour over the pears. Add the vanilla bean and cloves.

2. Cover the pan and bring the liquid to a simmer over medium heat. Simmer, partially covered and turning the pears occasionally, about 30 minutes, until the pears are cooked through and evenly colored. Remove the pan from the heat and let the pears cool in the liquid. Transfer the pears and their liquid to a glass or ceramic bowl. Cover and refrigerate 24 hours before serving.

Makes 6 servings

Grilled Peaches with Raspberry-Port Sauce

Grilled peaches are sweet and slightly smoky tasting, and the perfect foil for a sweet port sauce. This is a nice way to end a dinner from the grill, because by the time the coals burn down to a dull red with a thick covering of ash, dinner will be over and you and your guests will be in the mood for a light dessert.

Prep time: 15 minutes Grill/Cook time: 20 minutes

Raspberry-Port Sauce:
2¹/₂ cups fresh raspberries
¹/₂ cup sugar
¹/₂ cup water
¹/₂ cup port

Grilled Peaches:
6 small peaches, peeled, pitted, and halved
2 tablespoons fresh lemon juice

1. To make the sauce: Combine the raspberries, sugar, water, and port in a medium saucepan; bring to a boil over high heat. Using the back of a wooden spoon, mash the berries against the side of the pan as the mixture reaches a boil. Reduce the heat to low and simmer, stirring often, about 5 minutes, until the berries are very soft. Press the berry mixture through a fine sieve into a large bowl. Discard the solids and seeds. Return the sauce to the saucepan and cook over medium heat, stirring, about 5 minutes, until thickened. (The sauce can be cooled to warm room temperature, covered, and refrigerated for up to 2 days; warm gently over low heat before serving.)
2. To prepare the peaches: Toss the peach halves with lemon juice. (The peaches can be prepared to this point, covered, and refrigerated for 2 to 3 hours.)
3. Prepare a medium-hot gas or charcoal grill. Lightly oil the grill rack. If using charcoal, let the coals burn until they are covered with a thick layer of gray ash and are glowing red.
4. Lay the peaches, cut sides down, on the grill and cook for about 5 minutes, until the cut sides are golden. Turn and cook 3 to 5 minutes longer, until heated through. Serve the peaches with the warm sauce spooned on top.

Makes 6 servings

Minted Fruit Salad

There is nothing better than a summer fruit salad made with fresh peaches, plums, and melon—all at the peak of freshness. Even better: Add a dollop of mixed yogurt and sour cream and a drizzle of honey.

Prep time: 30 minutes plus chilling

3 ripe peaches, peeled, pitted, and sliced

6 small ripe plums, pitted and sliced

1/2 ripe melon, such as honeydew, cantaloupe, or Crenshaw,
    seeded and cut into 1/2-inch cubes or balls (about 2 cups)

1/4 cup chopped fresh mint

1 cup plain low-fat yogurt

3 tablespoons low-fat sour cream

Honey, for drizzling

Mint leaves, for garnish

1.   Place the peaches, plums, melon, and mint in a large bowl and toss together. (Note that the flavor of mint intensifies over time. If you prefer a less minty flavor, add the mint to the salad about an hour before serving.) Refrigerate for about 2 hours.

2.   Line a sieve with a coffee filter or cheesecloth and place over a bowl. Spoon the yogurt into the filter and let drain 15 minutes. Transfer the yogurt to a small bowl. Add the sour cream and mix well. Refrigerate until ready to serve.

3.   Spoon the fruit salad into dessert bowls or plates. Top each serving with a spoonful of the yogurt mixture and drizzle with honey. Garnish each serving with mint leaves and serve.

Makes 6 servings

Serving Style

An afternoon tea or a buffet dessert party is a great way to entertain during the hectic holidays—or any other time of year. Let your guests serve themselves from a selection of cakes, cookies, and other indulgent sweets while you pour freshly brewed coffee and tea.

CASUAL TABLEWARE

White china coffee cups, mugs, and dessert plates set the right tone for an afternoon dessert party with friends.

fresh whipped cream

There is nothing better with a bowl of fresh berries or fruit than a dollop of freshly whipped cream. It's simple to make—all you need is a cup of heavy cream and a teaspoon of sugar. Put the cream in a large bowl, add the sugar, and whip with a whisk or hand mixer until the cream is just stiff.

Additions to whipped cream that impart extra flavor are a tablespoon (or two) of rum, bourbon, or fruit brandy—just delicious over cakes, pies, tarts, and cobblers.

acknowledgments

My thanks go to:

The people at Sterling Publishing Co., Inc., Pam Horn, Christine Byrnes, Teryn Kendall, and Heidi North, for helping make this book happen.

Colin Cooke, for his wonderful photography, Andrea Kapsales, for food styling, and Phyllis Asher, for her amazing prop styling.

My friends and family, all gracious dinner guests and tough critics, with whom I have shared good food and great times at the table over many years

metric equivalents

The recipes in this cookbook use the standard United States method for measuring ingredients (teaspoons, tablespoons, and cups). If you need to convert to other measurements, use the charts below. All equivalents are approximate.

Equivalents for Liquid Ingredients By Volume

U.S.							Metric		
1/4 tsp	=						1 ml		
1/2 tsp	=						2 ml		
1 tsp	=						5 ml		
3 tsp	=	1 tbls	=		1/2 fl oz	=	15 ml		
		2 tbls	=	1/8 cup	=	1 fl oz	=	30 ml	
		4 tbls	=	1/4 cup	=	2 fl oz	=	60 ml	
		5 1/3 tbls	=	1/3 cup	=	3 fl oz	=	80 ml	
		8 tbls	=	1/2 cup	=	4 fl oz	=	120 ml	
		10 2/3 tbls	=	2/3 cup	=	5 fl oz	=	160 ml	
		12 tbls	=	3/4 cup	=	6 fl oz	=	180 ml	
		16 tbls	=	1 cup	=	8 fl oz	=	240 ml	
		1 p	=	2 cups	=	16 fl oz	=	480 ml	
		1 qt	=	4 cups	=	32 fl oz	=	960 ml	
						33 fl oz	=	1000 ml	= 1l

Equivalents for Cooking/Oven Temperatures

	Fahrenheit	Celsius	Gas Mark
Freeze Water	32° F	0° C	
Room Temperature	68° F	20° C	
Boil Water	212° F	100° C	
Bake	325° F	160° C	3
	350° F	180° C	4
	375° F	190° C	5
	400° F	200° C	6
	425° F	220° C	7
	450° F	230° C	8
Broil			Grill

Equivalents For Dry Ingredients By Weight

(To convert ounces to grams, multiply the number of ounces by 30.)

1 oz	=	1/16 lb	=	30 g
4 oz	=	1/4 lb	=	120 g
8 oz	=	1/2 lb	=	240 g
12 oz	=	3/4 lb	=	360 g
16 oz	=	1 lb	=	480 g

Equivalents for Length

(To convert inches to centimeters, multiply the number of inches by 2.5.)

1 in	=					2.5 cm	
6 in	=	1/2 ft	=			15 cm	
12 in	=	1 ft	=			30 cm	
36 in	=	3 ft	=	1 yd	=	90 cm	
40 in	=					100 cm	= 1 m

index